THE TATE BIBLE

ANDREW TATE

G. SLIM

COBRATATE

Arranged and edited by G. Slim

thegslim@gmail.com

cobratate@gmail.com

CONTENTS

THE TATE'S PRAYER

Our Tate, who art in Bucharest,
Andrew be thy name;
Thy kingdom come;
Through cam and fun;
Online as it is on the blockchain.
Give us this day our daily vodka,
And forgive those, the shit-munchers,
For their trespasses against us.
Lead us to women for temptation;
And deliver unto us our Dominos;
For his is the Lambo, the McLaren, and Ferrari
For ever with Tristan.....Amen

HOW THIS BOOK CAME TO BE (DISCLAIMER)

During the first Covid lockdown in the UK, I was sat around, scrolling through Twitter.

I had never seen nor heard of Andrew Tate before, but someone I follow must have re-tweeted him.

I remember reading the tweet and laughing at it, so I went to his @OfWudan Twitter profile and had a look through the posts.

It was incredible. Who the fuck was this guy? Was he for real, or was it a parody account?

For the next hour or so I did nothing but scroll through his tweets.

And these weren't just singular tweets like your average person posts, but long threads that I got lost in. They flew from subject to subject, dropping controversy, humour, and pearls of wisdom alike.

I won't lie to you, I genuinely still thought it was a parody account. I could not believe anyone actually thought like this. Surely it was a wind-up?

And so I closed Twitter and went about my day. But the thing was....I couldn't stop thinking about it.

At the back of my mind a realisation had started. A thought that actually, this guy was the real deal. It wasn't a joke. It wasn't some prankster trolling everyone.

So the next day I found his YouTube channel, and fell down the biggest fucking rabbit hole in existence.

Tatespeech, The Hateful Tates, The War Room, Tate Confidential. Over the next few months during lockdown, I would dip in and out of all this content.

And on this journey of discovery I noticed one thing kept popping up in the comments.

"Tate, you should write a book".

Several times I saw this. And when he bothered to reply, Andrew would scornfully say the same thing: "I ain't got time to write a book, I'm too busy driving a McLaren through The Alps!"

You can't argue with that.

But something clicked in my head. As someone who had rapidly consumed most of the Tate media in a short time, I realised that he had already written a book. It's just that no-one had put the pages together yet.

And then the lessons that I'd heard him preach time and time again came crashing in:

Ideas! Action! Speed! A fucking PLAN!

I decided right there and then, that I was going to write the book.

I needed to be in this man's circle. I needed to be in the War Room. I needed to change my life.

I needed a fucking LAMBO!!!

LET'S DO IT!!!

And then in the next days....nothing.

That little doubting voice that tells you you'll never be able to do it, appears in your head.

Who the fuck are you to try and do this?

You've never written a book in your life, what are you thinking?

Tate hates books. He's gonna laugh in your face.

You're gonna waste all your time doing it, it'll never work out.

It took me weeks of questioning myself to even get started. And even then I stopped halfway and thought long and hard about whether I should continue.

But am I going to be a loser? Am I going to fail to follow through? After all, what's the WORST that can happen? He might tell me to fuck off, and I realise i've wasted my time.

But I can handle that.

What I CAN'T handle is always thinking what *might* have happened if i'd finished it and it all works out.

What if a year later, someone else does it and it's a huge success?

So from that moment I became a "Sayer". You'll find out what a "Sayer" is later in this book. But essentially I *SAID* I was going to do it out loud.

And so I had to do it.

Otherwise I was going to be some weak-willed loser.

I could live with the failure and rejection. But I couldn't live with that.

I decided I would complete the book in total secrecy, and then get a physical paperback version printed to give to him. This, I hoped would get the seal of approval.

So I began the long and arduous task of reading every tweet he'd ever posted, and watching every video he'd ever made

AGAIN. But this time finding the best bits, and transcribing them.

So, these transcripts have been edited for clarity and brevity, sometimes several times, as I attempt to present Andrew in his own words as closely as possible. Occasionally chapters will seem to contradict themselves in regards to his claims about the amount of money, women, cars etc he might be talking about. This is purely because the information is not sorted by date order, but rather to present a better narrative.

As the content moved through time and space, some phrasing may have changed in order to present it as he originally intended. Some things have been edited for readability.

Many parts are pulled from interviews, and I have tried where possible to either show the interview flow, or present the text as a stream of thought.

The book doesn't have to be read in order. You can jump about as you wish.

All brilliance in this book is Andrew's; any mistakes are mine.

G. Slim 2021

*"My unmatched perspicacity,
coupled with sheer indefatigability,
makes me a feared opponent in any realm of human endeavour"*

Emory Andrew Tate

THE TRUTH ABOUT YOUR EGO

W e're going to be talking about ego and why it's super important that you have an ego. In fact, the biggest worms I've met in my life are people who don't have egos. If you don't have an ego, you don't care about how you're perceived. And there's not only how you're perceived by others, but you also don't care about how you perceive yourself.

IF YOU'RE GOING to become morbidly obese, you don't have an ego. You can't have an ego and become a morbidly obese person. Now, I think a lot of people get confused because there's two types of egos. You've got people who have egos who don't deserve, it and people who have egos who have earned it and justified it. Mike Tyson had an ego. He's Mike Tyson.

Mike Tyson
   "*There's never any doubt in my mind because I'm the best in the world, even though a lot of you don't like to hear it. It's fact. I'm the*

best. *Sometimes I don't want to believe it myself, but it's the truth. I'm the best. How dare they even challenge me, these fighters? You know what I mean? With their primitive boxing skills. You know what I mean? They're as good as dead."*

"I'm the most brutal and vicious and most ruthless champion there's ever been. There's no-one can stop me. I'm the best ever. There's never been anybody. There's no-one that can match me. My style is impetuous. My defence is impregnable, and I'm just ferocious. I want your heart. I want to eat his children."

So THERE NEEDS to be some kind of diversification in the words. We need to come up with some kind of word. Someone out there who is a master of the English language, you have to come up with a difference in the two sides of egotistical. Because egotistical, when it's justified and when it's not justified are different things.

And this can be an argument of proof and blah, blah, blah. But whatever. That's not the point.

I'm discussing egos of people who deserve them, people who have justified their ego like I have justified my ego. And I do have a massive ego. I like me and I like that I am me.

I think I'm the fucking man. I think I'm cool as fuck, and I'm happy with that. And I'm happy to live my life this way because I find it a source of motivation.

I would never let myself get out of shape because then I couldn't view myself the same. I view myself a particular way, and that requires me to be in shape.

I would never allow myself to become poor because I view myself a certain way, and that requires me to have financial assets. I view myself in a way that requires me to push hard to succeed, and it makes my life better.

. . .

PEOPLE OFTEN TALK about downward spiral. He got in a downward spiral. He lost his girlfriend, then he started drinking, he lost his friends, and he drunk more. You know what else is real? An upward spiral. You start training more, so you have more energy and start working more, start making more money. Than you go to a better gym and then you trained harder, and then... An upward spiral is exactly the same. An upward spiral is always fuelled by ego. So an ego is not a bad thing.

In fact, I encourage every man out there to have an ego, develop an ego, a massive one. And then work to justify it. It doesn't matter what it is. You can name any job in the world. Even a fisherman. If you have an ego and you really, truly believe you're the best fisherman there is, you're gonna go out there and try to catch the best motherfucking fish. You may stay out longer than everyone else. You may try harder than anyone else, maybe try new baits. You may get up earlier, whatever it takes. But you want the biggest fish to prove you are the man. Doesn't matter what it is. If you're doing anything creative, if you really believe you're the best, you're gonna put more energy into that creative art than if you don't believe you're the best. I love egotistical people. I love people with huge egos because they try hardest, and they try hardest to justify them.

Then you have the other side of the coin. The people have an ego for no reason, I wouldn't call this an ego. I'd call these people delusional. Morons.

And if you're going to go through your life and you have to associate with people, what you want to do is find egotistical people. Find out if they have a reason to justify their egos. if they can't, then get rid of them. If they do, then hang around them, because you might actually learn something.

～

DO GIRLS LOVE MONEY?

A lot of people say girls love money, and that's not entirely true.

They think that if you have money you're gonna get girls, but it's incorrect.

I know loads of very rich men who don't have girls, and I know loads of old, fat, ugly, rich guys who are desperately trying to throw money at girls, and these girls won't fuck them because they don't really care about money.

Girls like the trappings of money without seeing the actual money. A girl doesn't want you to sit there and say you earned this much, and that you have this and that. They don't give a fuck.

WHAT THEY WANT IS a black Mercedes to pick them up from their house, to take them to the restaurant. Then you pay the bill without mentioning how much it is, and a black Mercedes to take them home again afterwards. Or they jump in your Lambo and go back to your penthouse and fuck.

They don't give a shit how much your heating bill is. They

don't care how much the taxes are on your big-ass apartment. They just want your bed to be big and comfortable. They want the trappings of money without the details of how money is made.

ANOTHER THING FEMALES enjoy is men who are successful, And money's a very easy measure of success. On top of that, the number one thing women want more than anything, is fun. Women like fun. You can do anything you want to a woman, you can even be horrible, but do not bore her. As long as you do not bore a female, and you're entertaining enough for her to have some enjoyment in her life, she will always be around.

This is why women often like funny guys for example.

Women like fun. And money facilitates spontaneity, and spontaneity is fun.

When you can say to a chick "We're going to Disneyland today" without having to worry about the money, then you're going to be more likely to have females around you than if you couldn't afford to do such a thing.

They don't necessarily love money, they're not gold digging, but rather because you're just a fun person to be around. They're driving about in the Lambo, and they're in a helicopter, and they're in Disneyland, and all of a sudden oops, they're sucking dick.

This is how it works with women and money. Women are not attracted only to money, they're attracted to all the things that money provides. And this is why women are kind of contradictory, because they say they don't care about money, and they're not lying.

Showing them the figure on your bank screen doesn't impress them. They don't give a shit.

However, if you don't have a car, you don't have a house, and you ain't got shit, she ain't gonna want to bang you. She just doesn't realise that money is the link to all the things she actually does want. There's the contradiction.

So when people remark to me that I have money so I get girls, I say "Well yeah obviously."

Because i can facilitate spontaneity. I have some very nice things, and i'm a successful individual.

But it only helps. Money alone is not enough to get girls. If you're just thinking that if you get money girls will like you, then you're mistaken. They won't.

LET me tell you something about having a Lamborghini. It's 200 thousand dollars to buy, 10 thousand dollars a year to service, 11 thousand dollars a year in insurance. Forget that i've replaced the windscreen twice this year from stone chips, which is another 10 thousand dollars. Forget the miscellaneous costs. It's about 3 hundred to 4 hundred thousand dollars i spent so far on a car that has no guarantee of getting girls.

But what it does do, is if i pull up outside of a nightclub in my Lamborghini, then girls look at me and think "Well i don't see that kind of car very often, that's interesting. Who is he, how does he afford a Lamborghini?"

If I continue to talk to a girl I have about 20 to 30 seconds to say something interesting and continue to be an interesting person, otherwise i'm going to lose her.

What it does is it facilitates an opener. It gets a tiny bit of interest but it's still my job to finish the interest off.

If I'm a boring cunt and she asks "How'd you get a Lambo?", and I sit there and go...

"Well the Lamborghini has a V10 5.2 litre engine...." She doesn't give a fuck about the fucking engine in the car. If a girl sees your Lamborghini it gives you an opener.

She's more interested in who you are and how you can afford a Lamborghini, but it's your responsibility to be interesting thereafter. All it gives you is 10 to 15 seconds of interest that you wouldn't have otherwise. That's what three hundred thousand dollars buys you. But if you don't have game after that, then you're still not going to get her.

You're not going to get girls purely because you have a Lambo. Girls don't give a fuck.

They don't care.

Let me tell you what you get if you buy a Lamborghini: the only people who genuinely adore you when you have a Lamborghini are 10 year old boys.

They see it drive past, and their eyes light up, and they start waving their hands, and they'll do anything to get in your car.

So unless you're a paedophile, there's no point buying a Lambo to get pussy.

Buy it because you enjoy it yourself. And this once again goes to the point that money is a facilitator.

Money helps, but you still need game to get girls.

That's absolutely one of the most important things I've said to people.

These weak men say "Well if I get money then I'll have girls."

No you won't.

You won't have girls. You're still out shape, still a fucking loser, you're still fucking boring. So fix all those things first.

Let me tell you something - If you fix all those things well enough, then you don't even need money to get girls.

I had girls when i was broke, and I have girls now i'm rich. I got my Lambo because I enjoy it, not to impress some bimbo bitch.

～

50 THINGS EVERY MAN SHOULD DO

1   Have a professional fight.
It'll teach you a lot about yourself.
Stuff you don't want to know. Stuff thats hard to accept. Stuff you either fix, or pretend you never learned, because it's not something you can LIVE with.

2.

Have your heart broken and don't say a word.
Don't tell your friends. Don't tell the girl. Don't tweet about it. Don't mention to anyone EVER.
Be a MAN about it.
Don't end up bitter and hate-filled like these red-pill dorks over the woman who left them.
Just move on.

3.

Retire your mother.
I have super cars and 4 x world titles and millions of

dollars... But the thing Im most proud of is when I told my mother she didn't have to work anymore.

4.

Work for an entire week and give all of the money away.
You need to change your attitude towards money.
Those who hoard money never enjoy life.
Savers live shit lives. And you only live once.
Give it to a dogs charity, dogs have pure hearts.
Fuck the money. Make more.

5.

Drive a supercar around Europe with your best friends.
Ferrari in Italy
Porsche in Andorra
Lambo in St Tropez
Some of my best memories are laughing hysterically with my brother while driving a beautifully engineered vehicle - on my way to a 5 star hotel in the mountains.

6.

Reject sex from a beautiful woman.
The red-pill dorks are desperate for sex. At my level, you refuse to let a woman have you simply because she's beautiful.
She has to deserve a man like me.
I reject stunning women all the time. It's good for the soul.

7.

Tip enough to become someones "biggest tip ever" story.

There are at least 100 servers in the world, when asked about their largest ever tip.. will say my name.

8.

Fly first class and don't sleep.

Drink a lot of champagne and eat a lot of food and watch bullshit movies.

Be extra friendly to the cabin crew.

Enjoy the experience for what it is... an experience.

9.

Survive by charm alone.

When I was a fighter, before I had a cam company. I had a nice car, but no house.

However, I had 4 girlfriends. They had houses.

They also had food. And pussy.

I didn't have a house for a year, but I slept, ate, and fucked just fine every single night.

10.

Eat a completely shit diet for a month.

Live on all the complete junk that tastes good but is bad for you. All the stuff you want when you're dieting.

Then notice how you feel. Realise some people LIVE this way, and you'll understand why so many are so unhappy.

11.

The opposite of the previous point.

Fast.

Be hungry and don't bitch about it.

In fact, fast, and don't tell anyone. Don't mention it. Don't tweet it.

JUST DO IT.

Nobody cares anyway. So shut up.

12.

Have kids.

Why else are you alive?

Why else are you learning? If you have no one to teach?

Every man should aim to have children.

But don't let your life end because of it.

Continue being you and maintain your freedom.

13.

Tell someone to fuck off mid-sentence.

This quickly becomes a habit.

It's better for you, it's better for them. It's better for everyone.

Like ripping off a bandaid.

It's something not many men do often enough.

You're thinking it... so say it.

14.

Admit you were wrong but don't say sorry.

"I was wrong but I did what I believed was the best thing to do at the time.

I cant be sorry for doing the best I could possibly do.

If I went back in time, Id do the same thing again.

So no. I am not sorry. Even if I was wrong"

. . .

15.

Get arrested.

A couple nights in jail is good for you.

I've accumulated about two weeks across different incidences.

I think that might just be the perfect amount.

16.

Next time your phone breaks, or you lose it....

Wait a week before you buy a new one.

Yes I know, work money bla bla bla.

Wait a week.

All of a sudden the real world is interesting again.

Conversations. People. They suddenly matter.

Its pretty amazing.

17.

Dig a hole big enough to stand in.

It's good for your upper body.

It takes resolve and will.

And it's a reminder of where you're going to end up.

Once the hole is dug, fill it up - and go LIVE YOUR LIFE.

18.

Forgive someone who badly wronged you.

Forgiving people is a skill which can be learned.

The only way you can stop giving a fuck, is to forgive.

Do not ALWAYS forgive.

But there is a time, and a place, to just let it go.

.   .   .

19.

There is also a time and a place for merciless revenge.
Choose accordingly.
There is no in-between. No grey.
Only black and white.
Destroy their life.
Or forget they ever wronged you.
Do not live in-between.

20.

Ask your parents what would make them happy, and do it.
Stop being an ungrateful dickhead.
Usually, you'll find, they're very happy you even asked at all.
And they don't want ANYTHING except for YOU to be happy.
Now you can do whatever you want and EVERYONE is happy.

21.

Get a loan and refuse to pay it back.
Sell or transfer your assets first.
Or do it just before you move country.
Cash enslaves people. It's not fair.
The banks are absolute criminals and you need to get some small retribution.
They'll simply print more money. Fuck them.

22.

Become very good at stealing.
I never ever order a coffee from Starbucks without stealing something from the front right under the dickhead's nose.

Never steal from small business. Steal from the huge multi
nationals who don't pay tax.

23.

Buy a plane ticket the same day it takes off.
Who cares if it's more expensive.
It makes the whole thing more exciting.
You'll see.

24.

Send a hand written letter when you could have sent an
email.
Especially to old people.
They love letters.
Also - you'll be amazed how shit your hand writing is.
Try and make it neat.

25.

Fuck your girl's best friend.
Females have absolutely zero loyalty to each other.
Seriously zero.
Fuck her best friend, then keep your original girl.
Now her BF who always says to dump you, is gone.
Problem solved.

26.

Completely change your sleeping pattern and live a month
absolutely nocturnal.
Amazing for productivity.
There isn't much open to waste time with at 4am on a

Tuesday.

27.

Move into a new apartment.
Contents:
A bed. A laptop.
One plate, one cup, one fork.
Stay this way for a month.

28.

Sleep outside.
No tent.
Just get a sleeping bag, on a dry day - and sleep outside.
Sun will have you up nice and early.
Plenty of time for exercise.

29.

Go to a casino.
Get a little bit of money, fuck around and waste time.
Watch the others play. Watch some win big, lose big.
Watch the excitement on one man's face.
The other man's look says "I'm fucked, I can't pay the rent"
Watch everyone win and lose.
Enjoy the stories.

30.

Be everywhere 15mins early NO EXCUSES for an entire month.
Guarantee you'll never be late for anything ever again.
Being late - is disrespect.

If you wanna get far in life, you'll meet important people.
You can never, ever, ever, be late.

31.

Get a passport, bank account, drivers licence in a foreign country.
Get a residence in a foreign country.
Sit on it.
Because one day....

32.

Choose a book about a story that sounds interesting.
A man who's travelling around Africa.
Or a man who decided to sail the Mediterranean.
A professional boxer.
Whatever.
Throw the fucking book away and go do it yourself.
Live > Read

33.

Pay for the toll for the car behind you.
Tell the toll attendant to tell the car you already paid and that you remember them from school.
Drive as fast as you can.
I guarantee they'll try and catch you to see who you are.
Enjoy the race.

34.

Compliment the chef at a buffet.
NOBODY ever compliments a buffet chef.

Imagine being a chef 15 years without a single "This is good!"

He was trying for nothing but now his life has purpose again.

35.

Say what you would say at their funeral to their face before they die.

While they can still hear you.

36.

Go to Rodeo Drive.

Go SERIOUS window shopping.

Make a detailed list of all the things you want that you cant afford.

Cut that list of 100 down to a list of 5.

Realise that you never really wanted the other 95 anyway.

Apply this to everyday purchases.

37.

Develop a poker face. A real one.

This is essential for a man. Pro fighting and chess taught me mine.

It saved my life in Jamaica

And if you THINK you have one, you don't.

99.9% of men don't.

LEARN this. Immediately.

38.

Drive a supercar on ice.

Drive around a race track in reverse.

Learn to drift.

I have done these things. Plus A LOT more.

I am an exceptional driver. Because I train. I study it.

All men THINK they can drive.

Be one of the few that REALLY can.

39.

Threesomes are absolutely over-rated.

However, there is a skill to having sex with multiple women at once.

Before you know it, it's you and 5 women. Tristan has the record with 6.

"Im not Bi" she said.

"You're not having sex with each other. You're all having sex with me."

40.

Sit with your closest friend and talk about all the things that went wrong.

All the times you could have died.

That car that almost crashed, the time you were almost stabbed.

Imagine how many CLOSE CALLS you managed to survive to end up right here, right now.

Then smile.

41.

Stick to your word even if there is zero foreseeable benefit for doing so.

It's always worth it, in the end.

. . .

42.

Take 100 dollars from your pocket.

Stop being a selfish dickhead.

Go and buy a ton of pepperoni and take a long walk.

Feed every stray dog you see.

I guarantee there is no afternoon that will make you feel happier.

It'll be the best 100 bucks you ever spent.

43.

Stop cowering to the machine.

They are not as powerful as you imagine them to be.

Tell the tax man you didn't earn any money, and you don't have any money, and you're sorry.

Worst case, you pay him.

You'll be surprised how far "Dunno, i'm broke" gets you.

Billionaires do it.

44.

Test your friends.

Say you need a place to stay for a month.

One month. Grab the couch. Clean up after yourself. Be a good guest.

Make sure they have zero excuse to kick you out.

So when they DO kick you out (his girlfriend told him to) you KNOW he's a bitch.

45.

Make the decision to stop taking medicine unless it's life threatening or an antibiotic.

Popping that pain pill every time something hurts a little, is bad for your mental strength.

DEAL with it.

And as above... do not mention you have a headache.

NOBODY cares.

46.

Stop yourself using excuses for anything ever, no matter how valid.

STOP saying them, and eventually you'll STOP thinking them.

"Did you crash the car"

Yes, it was icy

The car is still crashed. The excuse repairs nothing.

You failed. Accept it. Learn

Don't do it again

47.

I gave a 100 dollar bill to every single homeless person I saw when I was in Austin, Texas.

Guess how many times I filmed it?

Zero.

Buying attention is not the same as charity.

Do not respect the former. It's selfish bullshit. Cheap social media likes.

48.

Learn to understand a foreign language.

Tell nobody.

Listen.

LISTEN more and SPEAK less in general anyway.

Nobody is impressed with your broken bullshit Spanish. Just speak English. But LISTEN.

"Oh sorry I don't speak Romanian"

I know exactly which girl wants to fuck who.

49.

Be the father/brother to somebody who lost their father/brother.

50.

Think back on some of your biggest arguments you've had and realise you were actually wrong for a few of them.

Not all. But some.

Remember this next time you're in an impassioned argument.

Theres always a chance that you're fucking up.

∾

LAWS OF THE PIMP GAME

Beautiful women work for me and make me millions of dollars.

They obey me because they love me. They clean my house and make me coffee and get naked on demand.

That's how I make over 300k a month. I own a webcam studio. It's no secret. I've never tried to hide it.

"THATS UNETHICAL" cry dorks. But the girls are rich, and I am rich. The girls sit on a computer and make huge sums of cash - no man touches them except me.

The men who spend their money on the sites do so willingly.

Everybody's happy.

Especially me.

THIS IS how I am rich.

I have a business which is generating money 24 hours a day at 100% profit. A business most men CAN'T do. And that's why they pretend it's offensive.

I don't gorilla pimp my girls, I don't force or hurt anyone.

I'm nice, and they're VERY nice to me. You could do the exact same thing. The USA or U.K. is even better than Eastern Europe to run this kind of business. The girls are more stupid.

Most men will SPEND money hanging around with hot girls.

But I EARN money hanging around with hot girls.

Yeah but "TATE'S A PIMP, TATE'S A SEX TRAFFICKER, TATE'S EVIL, REEEEEEEE"

No, Tate's got multiple super cars and casinos.

Tate gets a massage from 3 women at once.

Tate has 15 million LIQUID.

OUTSIDE of assets.

Don't worry about Tate.

Tates fine.

I HAVE BEEN EVERYWHERE in the world.

The choices to live are simple.

It's either Eastern Europe or South East Asia.

Nowhere else affords the safety/freedom combination. Let's do a break down between the two.

SEA is for everyone. Nobody is judged. They have every-thing a man needs at a reasonable price. Nothing bad will happen to you. Endless pussy and sunshine. Great food. Huge gyms and tons of activities. You'll never be bored or go broke. And that's 99% of life fixed.

EE IS VERY DIFFERENT. EE is a status society. Most dorks who move to EE don't realise this, because they have no status. But you can't come here and be a nobody.

If you aren't known - you won't enjoy it as much as SEA.

WHO you are. WHO your friends are. Are you above the law?

I love Romania because I can be myself in Romania. The average tourist here will never be able to do any of the things I can do. Also, EE has supercars and mountain roads. And that's a huge thing for me. I would miss cars too much if I lived in SEA.

AND EE HAS the most beautiful women in the world. However - they're hard to get. Much harder than western sluts. They won't fuck losers. Again - status. WHO ARE YOU?

Status talks absolutely in EE. If you move here, understand you need to become somebody. Fast.

South American women look like trolls compared to Moldovan women. Anyone who disagrees has never been to Moldova.

Trust me. EE is the best place in the world if you're important.

SEA second best if you're not looking to be street recognisable.

THE REST of the world is shit.

American girls won't even wear heels to the club. Bulgarian girls wear heels to go food shopping.

So, laws of the pimp game....

Based on my experience running 80+ webcam girls, 50+ Only Fans girls, and generating over $11,000,000 in turnover across 8 years. Living with multiple females for the past 6 years.

Let's go.

How did I start this company? It's a long story.

Short version.....

I was poor with many, many girlfriends, using them for

food and shelter. I decided I needed money, and found a way to monetise female beauty.

Which takes us into the first rule of the pimp game...

1.

Female beauty is the most valuable thing in the world. Wars were fought, and nations ruined - over a princess

The number one motivator for men to risk their lives in battle, was to be respected enough to have a beautiful woman.

Men used to DIE for beauty

Now they pay for it

Understand that a beautiful woman has value.

A 19 year old female, who's achieved basically nothing, and knows absolutely nothing...Is with a 45 year old millionaire who's smart and powerful.

The values are equal, ALL of his work = her beauty.

2.

If female beauty has a value, men SHOULD pay for it - every man except YOU.

I've never paid for sex in my life ever. I never will. I'll buy her dinner and take her somewhere nice. But I will not EXCHANGE money FOR sex.

One of the important things you do in the pimp game is change the woman's thinking.

Why are you talking to men you "like"?

They don't GIVE you anything.

You are special and men should PAY to talk with you.

Thats what YOU deserve.

I will HELP YOU.

Females throw their value away for free, all day long in return for bullshit jokes and "game".

As a pimp - you need good hoes - and HOES want to be PAID.

I have cam girls who have never replied to an instagram DM in years. I see their accounts.

They ignore ALL MEN unless PAID.

My women never fucked men. They only spoke to them online.

You have to change a woman's mind to understand a man doesn't exist in her world unless he's paying. Where does she get emotional support and connection? From the one man she can trust.

You.

3.

Your women must love you.

And sure, love them back. But you have to be ready for heart break.

"Bitches come and go, every nigga pimpin know"

I've lost over 75 women I WANTED to keep. And I never ever showed it, ever. Not even for half a second.

The pimp game is hard.

Girls get jealous. The customers come and go.

It's highly emotional. Some girls can't take it and bail, they start craving stability. If you show weakness when one leaves, the others will think about leaving. It will inspire mutiny.

When I was living with 15 women, and one would leave - me and the others would have a small party.

FDB party. "Fuck dat bitch party"

We would talk about how stupid she was to leave. What's she going to do now? Probably fall in love with some simp.

This was important..

I had many women who stayed because they were afraid of being the subject of an FDB party if they left. They had sat and ripped so many women for leaving. They didn't want to become what they once mocked. They'd rather share me with every other woman in the house and obey.

4.

Avoid gorillas and Godzillas.

Gorilla pimping - forcing a woman to do something - never lasts long. And it will put your ass in jail.

PIMP

Positively

Inspirational

Motivating

Person

Women need to WANT to work for you, or they won't do it.

How do you make a woman WANT to work for you?

I get this question endlessly.

WHY would a woman WORK for YOU? WHY would she give you MOST of her MONEY?

WHY not do it HERSELF and keep the money?

Any man who asks this question isn't a pimp. And never will be. She wants to work for me for the same reason you WANT to put gas in your car. You NEED the gas. And she NEEDS me. How could she do any of this without me?

What about the taxes? What about that day it was quiet online and I changed her room around and it got busy? What about that crazy customer who's scaring her? What about that forum that found out her real name?

WHO does she come to?

WHO has the answer every single time?

Her man.

Women cant handle the emotion of doing this alone.

They need a rock, and they need instruction.

If a woman truly respects you, she wants to be your robot. "Go here and do this"

I will handle the why and how. I will handle the problems. Just do this, at this time, this way. Go.

OH LOOK! YOU DID IT!

I am very happy with you.

They work to make ME smile.

They love me

For the same reason a simp will buy his wife an expensive gift.. a hoe will give a pimp all of her money.

The money isn't as valuable as the person they love being happy with them. They would rather me be pleased, than cash in the bank.

Which brings us to the next rule...

5.

You're either a PIMP or a HOE.

There is no in-between, there is no half of anything.

Your job's the pimp, the employee the hoe.

THIS IS LIFE.

If you're a square, and your woman will not obey your every command, and does what she "wants"... guess which one you are?

If a woman wouldn't obey me I didn't want to be with her.

I know more than she does.

I am infinitesimally more powerful.

Skilled and willed.

HOW can she NOT respect me enough to OBEY absolutely every command?

I will NEVER be a hoe, in ANY relationship

6.

Women are combative.

Women like to fight, because women enjoy attention. If a woman gets you to fight with her, you give her all of your attention.

Women love drama.

They watch the Kardashians all day.

THEY'RE ADDICTED.

USE THIS AGAINST THEM... how?

I had a little penthouse with my hottest girls. The ones I actually wanted to spend time with.

It would be me and three of them, fucking and watching TV. Chilling.

All would say in private "I wish we were alone sometimes. I'd do anything to be just us"

The girls would never fight. But they were always trying to get one up on the other - usually by pleasing me.

They were in direct competition.

Fate would have it that I fired two. And that last one left? Started arguing with me over dumb shit.

SHE BEHAVED when fighting the others.

But when there was no one left to fight with... guess who she turned on...

The drama and battle is simply too addictive to just behave themselves all of the time.

Theres a fine line, you have to make them ALL friends while ALL ratting on each other.

She felt powerless with those other two girls in the house.

She knew, they'd WANT her to fuck up, and she wouldn't give them the satisfaction.

But when they weren't there?

Why NOT be a dickhead now and again.

Do you understand?

.   .   .

7) WOMEN ARE ONLY loyal to one thing.

The dick they suck.

THAT'S IT.

You cant do a business deal with a woman. You cant come to an "agreement" If they don't fuck you.. they'll fuck someone else, and turn on you for him. EVERY SINGLE TIME.

If I wasn't having sex with a girl she would find a new man - and even though she could make great money with me, and have her separate boyfriend...

She wouldn't.

She would stop working for me because her man said so.

She'd quit her job and go broke. She would leave all her friends and her million dollar a year job because the new dick commanded her too.

FEMALES ARE loyal to absolutely NOTHING besides the man they WANT.

Not the man they have.. the man they WANT. They're not always the same thing.

UNDERSTAND this.

Therefore. Sex became a necessity.

Women want sex WAY more than men.

Men, If you don't find this to be true? You're bad in bed.

If you're good - they can never get enough.

The amount of sex a girl got from me was directly linked to how much money she made me

My dick isn't free

8.

You have very few weapons against a woman.

You can't hit her. What CAN you do? Get rid of her. Thats it.

Many men, don't use this weapon, as they know the woman won't care.

But that's because they're in a weak position.

If you're in charge - this is devastating. I would give multiple fair and calm warnings. I would rarely lose my temper - If i did, it was 0 - 1000 instantly.

Shock and awe. Throw her stuff and her laptop out of the window, and scream for her to get the fuck out of the house.

I didn't need my temper because girls feared it. Ultimately however, If a girl didn't comply she was replaced. Natural selection left the subservient, beautiful, kind females who obeyed.

The key to this was having new women everyday to test and train...

Which brings us to the next rule of the pimp game.

9.

She doesn't have to like you.

But she HAS to respect you.

And women always love men they RESPECT, even if they don't like him.

A lot of women hated me and loved me at the same time because they respected me.

They respected me because other men and other women respected me.

Every man I meet treats me with respect, any disrespectful female is banished.

When a female sees you involved in endless respectful interactions - she is going to respect you just the same.

If she sees a woman she KNOWS is better looking than her treat you like a king...

She's going to treat you like a king.

Even if she decides to leave - if she still RESPECTS YOU - she will do so peacefully.

If she doesn't respect you she will try to destroy your business, inspire other girls to quit, demand huge sums of money - and cause trouble.

10.

Women are an open book.

The idea that females are complicated is absolute fallacy.

They have zero stoicism.

When a woman is angry she acts angry.

Sad she acts sad.

Happy she acts happy.

They just wont tell you the reason WHY they feel this way.

All men know HOW a women feels, but a pimp knows WHY.

Never negotiate using logic as this never works.

Never explain WHY she should feel different.

Force her to feel different via circumstance, energy and persuasion.

Want her to obey?

Change her mood to change her mind.

She doesn't want to work 15 hours and then suck tits while you fuck her. Do you know why? Because she isn't happy enough today.

A pimp can MAKE his woman happy, near INSTANTLY with energy transfer.

Oh look.. she smiled, and she's horny. Funny that.

Positively inspiring and motivating person.

P.I.M.P.

If she feels good when she's with you, and she wants to make you happy - she will earn you money.

But a woman who would leave (under any circumstance) isn't a woman who's worth missing.

Therefore - a female can't win.

The second she leaves, I don't want her.

I would only want a woman who's good enough to stay.

Understand?

Once she realises you don't give a fuck - some stay proud and stick to their guns.

They get replaced.

They will think about you while you never think about them. Energy.

You've fucked 'em already anyway. Once or 100 times. Doesn't matter.

The game is rigged for men to win.

The only men who don't win - are loser men who miss a girl who's left.

HOW can you WANT a women who WOULD leave you?

She's NOT loyal? She's trash?

Replace

If you have nothing to eat you'll cry over a plate of food.

If you have no money you'll cry over 50 bucks.

If you have nothing to fuck you'll cry over a woman.

It's that simple.

～

I HAD A GUN PULLED ON ME

My brother and I are famous in Romania.

WE'RE ON TV, on every Romanian You-Tuber's channel, everybody knows us.

Its baffling to Romanians why two rich Americans would move here. Coupled with the super cars and Tristan's scandals with married singers. Famous. It's important for context.

DURING THIS VIRUS, everyone has abandoned the cities. The young people work in the big cities and all of the old people live in remote villages.

To hide from the virus, all the young girls (students etc) have gone home to their parents in remote villages around the country.

There was a girl I was dating and haven't seen for 7/8 months, who is in a remote village hiding with her parents.

.   .   .

WE STARTED SPEAKING AGAIN a week or so ago.

I told her I would come visit her, I felt like a drive - and Romania is amazing to tear around in a sports car.

I've driven ALL over Romania. Some roads are bad, some are amazing. There ARE speeding laws, strict ones, but you can negotiate your way out of them most of the time.

HOWEVER, I realised something today. I've always driven through villages that link major cities.

There are no highways in Romania. None. So if you want to go from one major city to another, you do it by passing through villages. These have very nice roads. They're the main transport routes for the entire country.

THIS village was in the middle of nowhere, and it led to nowhere. It has zero strategic importance.

And the roads were TERRIBLE.

This was a SHIT drive. The roads were FUCKED. Every time I got up to speed I had to dodge HUGE potholes.

Potholes that would DESTROY the car. 10 inches deep. For this reason, half-way through my drive - I was doing barely 30mph in the Mclaren. No fun at all.

EVENTUALLY I GET to the entrance to this village.

There is one road in. And one road out.

A police car at the entrance with two cops. Aged 60+ years old. Everyone in the village was old.

Nobody was in their houses.

They were all sitting outside on benches in the nice weather. Staring at the Mclaren like I was an alien. I had been there for 2 mins and now EVERYBODY knew I was there.

. . .

I PULL up to the girls house. She comes out.

She gets in the car and I tell her I need gas. There is one gas station for miles and she starts telling me the way. At 30mph we drive over potholes, and make small talk. College, school. Bullshit things.

She seems very happy. Everything is fine.

WE GET to the gas station...

I pull up. Press the engine button.

The Mclaren engine stays off, but the computer stays on. I get out of the car and begin to pump gas.

I MADE AN AMATEUR MISTAKE....

Because the car computer was still on, it was still connected to my blue tooth. Standing at the gas pump I open WhatsApp. 400+ messages. Usual story.

I start playing voice-notes from girls. Cant hear anything. Click play again. Not working.

Because the voice-notes are playing in the fucking car on the stereo. The girl is listening to them all.

I went to pay for the gas and then it clicked what I had done. I worked it out. WHY I couldn't hear them.

I BOUGHT TWO ICE-CREAMS.

Got back in the car and she's crying.

"I haven't seen you in months. Eat your ice cream", I say to her.

"I know you had girls, but it hurts me to hear this" she replied.

I opened my ice-cream and said i'd take her home. Its getting dark and I don't want to drive these shit roads at night.

She didn't reply. Just looked down, sad. I took her back to her house. She got out without saying goodbye.

I BLAST off down the road and out of town. Home time. I'm driving on the road out of town eating my ice-cream, and the police car is blocking the road. Sirens on.

"STOP STOP!", they shout.

I stop.

One officer pulls his weapon.

Listen, i've been pulled by police over 100 times. NEVER has a cop drawn on me before.

"OUT OF CAR" he shouts.

I get out of the car still eating my ice cream.

I AM FACING TWO OFFICERS. Two old men with wise eyes. They've been in the game a long time. The man closest to me is 1 metre away. The other a further metre back. He's the one with the weapon drawn.

I'm still eating my ice-cream.

They order me to show my empty palms then cross my arms. Different than the hands-up of the west.

I put the last bite of ice cream in my mouth, show empty palms and fold my arms.

The cop closest to me says "good."

Then he pulls out his phone to make a phone call. He begins to speak in Romanian on the phone

.   .   .

IT TURNS OUT, in this tiny village where everybody knows everybody, the father of the girl saw her crying when she came in, and called those cops.

He thought I'd hit her or hurt her. She ran to her room crying and didn't say what happenedThese cops don't speak english

"Girl cry. Girl cry. YOU. YOU!"

Pointing at me

I very calmly repeat "I don't understand." I speak extra slowly. Both of these men are mad. So I am as calm as a man can be, as if I was talking to a friend half-asleep on a beach

De-escalation tactics

Eventually the front cop takes the phone from his ear and hands it to me.

I take it.

It's her Dad.

He speaks English.

Him: "what happened?"

I tell him we're old friends, and she saw another girl in my phone so i took her home. A short simple version of the truth. No need to involve the bluetooth complications.

Him: "Yes. She tell me now. I don't like my daughter to cry"

Me: "Neither do I"

I hand the phone back to the cop.

THEY TALK FOR 30 SECONDS. He hangs up.

By now the gun-drawn cop has the weapon and his hand resting on his holster. Still pointing at me from the hip. Like a cowboy.

He lit a cigarette while the front cop says to me

"Cobra, Cobra. box box"

Yes, I replied.

Him: "Wait."

He calls another number and hands me the phone. It's his wife, who speaks English. The phone goes back and forth while his wife translates.

He asks me to teach his son kickboxing. His partner has a gun pointed at me. How can I say no? Five minutes of conversation later and it's all arranged.

On Sunday I'm returning to this village to teach 6 or 7 young boys how to kickbox in the main room at the police station. The cop shakes my hand then puts his hands up like a boxer.

I guess he fought in his younger years.

I took a drive to a tiny village, lost a girlfriend and gained a kickboxing class for redneck children. A one-off seminar.

I'll honour my commitment and teach them all.

The girl's last message - 'I heard you are teaching the kids. You are a good man but I can't see you again. Take care of you bb'. That's life.

∽

IMAGINE LIFE AS A MILLIONAIRE

I magine being a self made millionaire.

IMAGINE COMING from nothing - being given the same hours in your life as everyone else, and having used them to make your dreams come true, instead of wasting them smoking weed and watching reality TV.

Imagine understanding that money isn't important for buying possessions.

Sure, my Lambo is fun, but money is important to give you your freedom back. To give you your time back to do whatever you want to do. Not what you HAVE to do to pay bills.

Life is measured in seconds. You don't want to WASTE them WORKING.

IMAGINE BEING RETIRED AT 30.

Imagine never setting an alarm clock unless it's to catch a flight to a far flung destination.

Imagine people believing women are only with you for money, and that they don't really love you.

Imagine people failing to understand that beautiful girls don't care about money.

Instead they want a man who's spontaneous. A man who can message them all day, he doesn't need to work.

A man who can lay in bed with them all morning and stay up all night.

A man who can get them something they really want on their birthday.

A man who can make their problems go away. A man who says - you don't need a boss anymore, forget that coworker. Quit your job.

That all takes money.

They don't want a daily wage to be with you. They want to know their man makes their life better.

IMAGINE BEING the only man in a woman's life because you're the only man she needs. No boss. No friends. Nothing. You are the only male she ever interacts with.

Do you understand how much more a woman would respect you if you were EVERYTHING she needed.

IMAGINE your girl looking at you knowing she truly believes you're the best man in the world.

If she goes to work, and her male boss tells her what to do so she can earn some money because *you* don't earn enough, then there is another male who's above her in her eyes.

. . .

I TAKE care of my women. The only man who bosses them around is ME.

Imagine people on social media telling you that you pay for women to be with you instead of understanding why they really want you.

BUT CONSIDER THIS...

LESS THAN 1% of the worlds millionaires are below 40. And only half of them are single.

Men who can provide are in the top 0.5% of the most desirable men in the world.

So a woman wanting all those things is normal.

As is a man wanting a girl who's beautiful.

If you give a woman a life that makes her happy. Her love for you is real. I experience real love. You could change your life. But you don't. Only you know why.

AND THERE'S EVEN MORE.

Imagine driving a car so amazing that jealous people scream "rented" at you all day. But you know you paid for it in cash.

Imagine those people being stupid enough to think they insulted you in your Lambo while they stand at the bus stop.

Imagine having all the things money can't buy.

Strong. Healthy. With family and friends who you love.

TIME to train.

TIME to see friends.

MONEY IS IMPORTANT.

Imagine realising that when you have the three things all men want - money, women, and freedom.

You soon see people who don't have them send you hate. And all the other men who also have these things are your friends.

It's funny how envy works.

Hate = envy. Every time.

IMAGINE KNOWING your Dad died believing you were the greatest man on earth.

And being so immensely proud of you that it's all you ever discussed.

Imagine people telling you to be more tolerant. Because tolerant means having no opinion on anything.

Imagine listening to people's views knowing you have a genius IQ.

And they don't.

IMAGINE everyone telling you that having an ego is bad. When your own self belief is the only reason you made it. These are people who doubt themselves while I never did. Then they hate my ego. What they really hate is my self belief.

I STARTED a company and believed i'd make money.

I am a millionaire.

And I'll teach you to do the same.

They don't believe they can do it. They say your ego's too big. They work a job they hate for pennies. Why would I want to get rid of my ego and be like them?

They are everything I don't want to be.

Why should I care what they think?

. . .

IMAGINE TELLING your school teachers you don't need school because you are too smart to be told what to do, and then earning more per week than they do per year.

IMAGINE GIVING money to every homeless person you pass and not filming it for fucking Facebook likes.

Imagine tipping immensely and seeing hard-working waitresses beam with a smile knowing their work was appreciated.

IMAGINE NOTICING you've never once had hate from people as successful as you.

Only those who aren't doing as well. Remember what I said about envy. Over time. The greatest compliment you get is knowing others are envious.

IMAGINE people telling you not to talk about your success so much.

This is my LIFE.

My life is successful.

What else do I talk about on Twitter besides my own life?

That's what everyone talks about. You talk about TV shows. I talk about making money. It's our lives.

IMAGINE people telling you money isn't happiness and then watching them sacrificing their working hours and still failing to earn anything. Why are you doing what you HATE for money? If it isn't happiness?

Explain that.

. . .

IMAGINE OVERTAKING the man who's driving too slow and him screaming at you at the lights.

I'm sorry friend. My cars are worth more than 20 years of your salary.

My time is worth money, yours obviously isn't. Don't get mad I don't wanna do 29mph.

I have places to go. Imagine knowing he's not mad you drove fast - he's mad you have the car he will never have.

He's mad at himself and ENVIES you.

CASH = ENVY.

I promise you it's glorious.

Imagine knowing if he gets out his car and gets too fresh, you would knock him clean out with ease.

IMAGINE LIVING life and truly being happy with yourself.

Imagine having nights where you're too excited to sleep because life is so crazy.

Imagine not going to sleep until you're genuinely tired and not because you need to get up at a certain time. Spending a Wednesday morning watching the sunrise and sleeping all day because you weren't tired Tuesday night.

IMAGINE NEVER ARGUING with your partner over money. Imagine understanding the reason they don't teach financial planning in school is because it would stop everyone from going to university.

You finish in debt for a degree nobody cares about. Simply because you "didn't know what to do" when you finished college.

I'LL TELL YOU WHAT TO DO.

Copy and paste. Money. Forever.

Uni fees go up every year. More degrees exist every year (thereby lowering the value of a degree). You're paying more and more for something worth less and less.

IMAGINE TELLING people about your life.

The people you meet. The places you go. The women you spend your time with. The things you have. The memories you've made.

Imagine it being so different from their world that they call you a liar. Imagine people struggling to believe your life is really that good.

Imagine these same people telling you "YOU'RE UNHAPPY! BECAUSE YOU BRAG!"

Because they're unhappy and can't stand how happy you actually are.

IMAGINE NOT BELIEVING depression is a real disease.

Simply people living lives they don't want to live. Sure - I'd be depressed too if I worked in Starbucks and couldn't give the girl I love the life she deserves. Who wouldn't?

IMAGINE KNOWING you were a world level fighter. With pure grit and determination you did it because you saw someone do it on tv and believed you could do anything. PURE CONFIDENCE.

And because you didn't want to work in Starbucks.

IMAGINE you could get the best health care in the world for someone you loved at the end of their life.

Imagine looking back on your twenties knowing you spent the time earning money and competing in the hardest sport in the world.

Imagine being happy you don't look back on your past to see drunken nights and video games like most people do.

IMAGINE NEVER WANTING a Netflix subscription because you don't have time to waste watching box sets when you can afford to be living real life in the real world.

You've watched Breaking Bad from start to finish? I dedicated that time to racing cars on racetracks and climbing mountains. Who's more fulfilled?

IMAGINE KNOWING your children will grow up with the best possible life. Imagine not knowing the name of any celebrities because you don't want to live vicariously through anyone else. Your own life is too amazing to care about anyone else's. You don't care about them because they don't care about you. Imagine not supporting a football team or going to concerts for the same reason.

If I cared about music, I would learn the guitar and I'd be on the stage.

That's the kinda man I am.

I am the performer.

Not the idiot in the crowd with nothing who worships the performer. This is the difference between a real man. And everybody else.

Are you a man?

Next time you meet a man who "loves" his football team and doesn't try himself to get into the premiership... Make an instant judgement. Judge him as a follower. Judge him as weak.

Even if he failed to ever play for Arsenal. If he was a real man and loved football he'd be out there trying to get signed anyway.

TRY AND FAIL. We all fail. BUT WE DO NOT ALL TRY.

IMAGINE DRIVING through the council estate you grew up in with your brother in cars worth more than the houses.

Imagine looking in the mirror and being proud of yourself.

I will teach you EVERYTHING I know.

Imagine people saying you're obsessed with money. Imagine knowing you were a world champion because you were obsessed with kickboxing, and are a millionaire because you're obsessed with money. Imagine wondering why more people aren't obsessed with things that make their lives better?

IMAGINE HAVING NEVER EVER DONE a drug in your life.

Coke weed nothing.

Not even tried it.

Ever.

I love my reality. I don't try that hard to escape it. Imagine having a Hublot. A bank balance in the millions. Property all over the world. Matching Aston and Lambo. A 10/10 girl with no password on her phone

Then - some guy who hasn't got 10k saved, and who's girlfriend you could steal in 1.5 seconds telling you that you should be more humble. Should you should think like him?

It got him NOWHERE.

Imagine how much you laugh at his comments on your personality.

Imagine how much you don't want to be like him and would never take his "advice".

. . .

IMAGINE BROKE people saying money isn't happiness and thinking - how would you know?

IMAGINE smoking cigars with your brother on a tropical island knowing you could stay forever if you wanted.

You have no reason to go home.

And will never run out of money.

IMAGINE WRITING a Tweet and people correcting a grammar mistake because you typed it on your phone, and then them thinking they won while they get ready to go to work for fuck all cash while you sit with millions.

That's literally how stupid people are.

Imagine being 32 and having lived more life than most people ever will. Been to more places. Seen more. Done more. Earned more, spent more, fucked more, LEARNED MORE.

Imagine that person would teach you EVERYTHING they knew.

Imagine pointing out the truth and waiting for DM's full of hate from people who could never do what you have done.

IMAGINE THAT.

Change your life. Learn what I know here.

Even after I explain to them they've confused hate with envy.

They still can't help it.

If a man truly believes he can rip your head off with his little finger.

Whether you believe him or not.

You wouldn't want him to try.

Don't underestimate self belief.

I WAS TELLING people I'd be a millionaire when I didn't even have a car.

Not only am I a millionaire. I'm very GOOD at being a millionaire.

I drink the finest booze and eat the finest food.

The best cars. Luxury clothes, beautiful women, private jets. Six star hotels and chartered boats and unforgettable experiences.

I'm very GOOD at ENJOYING money

The average man doesn't try very hard.

So if you try very hard.

It's impossible to be average.

When I was broke I was unhappy. For some reason I thought if I can make enough money I'd be happy. I thought that if I had the most beautiful women, and the fastest cars, and total freedom, and knowing I did what everyone else fails to do - that i'd be fulfilled

AND I WAS TOTALLY RIGHT.

～

THE TATE BROTHERS

Andrew

Right. If you don't know who I am, where the fuck you been? I am Andrew Tate, four times kickboxing world champion, the world's sexiest man confirmed, a nice guy, millionaire, etc. People often ask me to do a podcast and I'm far too lazy. But that is coupled with people asking me loads of questions about my brother. So I decided I'm gonna interview my own brother, Tristan "The Talisman" Tate. It's super original never done before. That's what I do. I smash barriers. I'm a G.

So I have a list of questions here. I'm currently in one of my least favourite cities in the world, London. My brother is somewhere else, which is very unusual for us. So we're going to do an interview. So introduce yourself, Tristan.

Tristan

Tristan Tate, the better looking half of the Tate brothers. I've known you my whole life, surprise, surprise. I'm basically your teammate and sidekick in every single way. Every job you do, half the business is mine. Our house is half mine, our cars. We've worked as a team ever since we were teenagers, and we stopped punching each other in the face. And we've come really far together, which is why people are so interested in our relationship. So yeah, I'm happy. I don't know what questions they've been asking you, but I'm happy to divulge any information.

ANDREW

So what would you say to brothers who don't get along like we do? Why do you think we get along and other brothers don't get along as well as you and I?

Tristan

I think that you and I both have very unique personalities. I wouldn't give credit fully to us. Me and you are clones of dad. We've inherited a mindset which is from a very unique individual. And I think me and you both find it hard to make friends with people who don't share our mindset, and hard to find people who share our mindset in general. I think that brothers who don't work well together really need to reevaluate their life choices because you have to understand, even if you don't like your brother very much, who else but your brother are you going to trust around your women, around your money, driving your cars, etc? When I bought my first Range Rover, you crashed it and what was the first thing I asked you on the phone?

ANDREW

You didn't care about the car. You asked if I was all right.

. . .

Tristan

I asked if you were okay. Exactly. So brothers who are at each other's throats all the time can't work well together. That's fine. But you're not gonna get as far in life, and you're never gonna find someone you could trust as much as your brother. So I would reconsider your position.

ANDREW

What if we have a little scumbag brother who steals your money and doesn't listen and that shit?

Or if you have a little douchebag, a liberal?

Tristan

Jesus, I don't know. Well, I think it's the older brother's job, I guess, to try to influence the younger brother as much as he can. We left, we separated, living with mum full time. You were about ten. I was about eight, and I wouldn't say I was off the rails at all, but you did certainly have to teach me a lot of life lessons at age 13, 14, 16, 18, even as old as maybe 21, 22, until I could say I was my own man. There were a lot of lessons I looked to you for.

And that's not to say that I'm necessarily the student and you're the teacher. But you are the older one. You lived these things about two years before I did. You had your first girlfriend two years before I did. You got your driving license two years before I did. So a lot of lessons in life, you had to teach me and guide me. If your brother is a little dick head and he's so different from you and he's not the way that you want them to be as a little brother. Certainly. I mean, you failed, I guess, in your role as an older brother.

. . .

ANDREW

You whoop his ass. Fucking why? Who's protecting his bull-shit ideas? You need to go in there and kick his ass. And if your parents are sticking up for him being a little bitch, you just sit down and talk to your parents, too.

Tristan

I completely agree.

ANDREW

What's so wrong with people? Oh my little brother is a little retard. Give him an elbow on the top of his fucking head, correct him.

Tristan

And if it's your older brother who's a dickhead and you're actually smart and on the right path you know, it's still your job. Brothers are brothers. I look out for you. You look out for me. That's the way we've always been. You know, if you've got a best friend and you're saying shit like, "Oh, we're like brothers. Me and him are like brothers". You're not. You have to have a brother to benchmark it by and if you did, you wouldn't be saying that shit.

ANDREW

I agree completely. People like, "Oh, yeah me and my friends are like brothers". No you're not, you're all fucking liars.

So who do you think most people rely on then? They rely on their friends and their girlfriend. Why is that a bad idea? Because we're all social animals. Everyone needs someone. So when shit hits the fan or they really need help, then they call up their wife or they call up their friend or some shit. Why do you think that's not as good as me calling you to kick a hoe out the house or whatever I need you to do?

Tristan

Well, I think that's the problem. A lot of people, they seek companionship. Now me and you are never bored apart from, like, right now when we're not together. I mean, this is the highlight of my day. I'm drinking fucking gin and tonics. Talking to you is the highlight of my day. I'm bored as fuck when you're not around. The companionship that we have a lot of people seek. You know, if they want to go to the movies, they want to go on vacation. I always go everywhere with you.

I don't like even like taking fucking girls anywhere. They're boring as fuck. They have nothing interesting to say over dinner on the holiday, they just moan and wanna lay in the sun. The search for companionship. You can't get mad at people for it. And a lot of people don't have brothers. A lot of people don't have another option. But I would certainly say that you need to pick your companions wisely. And almost nobody does, because society lays out this plan for them on how to pick a companion, meet a girl, have sex with her, and that's your companion.

You need to buy a ring, you need to have a family and all that shit. And that's the worst way to find a real teammate. I mean, it's not like you're interviewed. It's not like it's a trial by combat, is it? It's literally she sucks on your dick and you come, and you think that's great and you suddenly think you found yourself a life partner. Well, these people are wrong. And I've seen so many men make the same mistake.

. . .

ANDREW

Yeah, I agree. Well, I'm gonna to elaborate on that. In general, I don't think females are good for helping you anyway. I can never think of a time I had a problem and I called a woman and told her my problem and the problem went away. I could literally never think of that. Unless I've got a boner that needs fixing. Besides that one issue I've never thought of the time I've called a girl and said, I've got this issue.

I need money, or fuck someone's out to kill me, or I've been stabbed or whatever. And a girl said something that wasn't just garbage. Women don't... They can't help with problems. The problem with having a wife as your partner and your teammate is, what the fuck can she do? Women are not combat ready. What could she do? Something's going down and you call your wife. She can't even drive there quickly without crashing the car. Like, what the fuck? She can't fight? They can't think for themselves.

So what is a woman good for? Besides for you to sit there and lament and cry about your issues, and you hope she's gonna give me some sympathy. If you're a little bitch and you want sympathy, then yeah, call a girl. Sympathy ain't fixing the problem. I don't want sympathy. I want solutions.

Tristan

I'll elaborate on that further. You're painting this picture of just women. This is at least 50% of men as well. I can think of people who I used to be let's say, friends with when I was 14, 15, 16. The video game playing weed smoking guys. And now I'm 30, 15 years later and they're still playing video games and smoking weed. They haven't moved on. But those are the kinds of guys you can't count on either.

They're gonna sit on the couch and be like, "Oh it's alright, man, come over. Let's have a drink". That isn't a solution to a problem. You're right. And most men are exactly the fucking same. You got to watch out for these people because they'll make you feel good. They'll make you feel good in the moment. Your girl will suck your dick, she'll give you a hug and you'll think, okay, everything's gonna be okay. Why? Nothing's gonna fucking be okay. She hasn't done shit.

ANDREW

True. A lot of men are like that and all women are like that. So that's why we hate the world.

When's the last time we argued?

Tristan

Last time, me and you probably had a serious argument is when I was 17 years old. As you know, I was working night shift at Luton Airport, so Storm Gym, the place where me and Andrew learned to fight, the place where we honed our skills, runs from 07:00, 08:00 p.m. for a couple hours. And that's when the training sessions were. So I was working night shift because I was making double the money.

But I was starting work at seven, eight. And then Andrew saying, look, you got to get off night shifts. Get back on the day shift so you can come and train at Storm Gym. I was like, "Nah, man, I'm making twice as much money. Look, I'm making £400 a week making fucking sandwiches". Yeah, I've done bullshit jobs too. And you told me, "No, you don't understand the importance of this training, the importance of being combat ready".

And we had an argument. It was maybe two or three weeks. We had a severe disagreement. I ended up turning off the night shifts and making less money, and going back on day shift so I could then pay money to train. But now as an older man, and this is an example of an older brother stepping in and guiding the younger brother, I understand the value of this is worth more than any money I could have made.

ANDREW
What would you have done with an extra 200 quid week at fucking 17?

Tristan
Probably went out and drank more.

ANDREW
Exactly.

Tristan
Coupled with not training. It is a recipe for disaster, it is a recipe for becoming the average man.

ANDREW
I was saying, we got to learn how to fight. We're gonna be out here as a team knowing how to fight. You can't be fucking around for a couple hundred pounds.
Fuck that. And you're right. I remember a huge argument you were telling me to fuck off.

Tristan
Cause I like the money. It was the same bullshit job. I doubled my wage. But you were 100% right. Because you have

to understand these people are going to the gym and training for vanity. Yeah, I mean, you look alright, but these people will often do things to their bodies to look good that make them zero-percent more combat effective. Now martial arts training and the way I see martial arts training and fight training, and me and you in this gym in my house now doing pads every morning with no upcoming fights or prospects of them, is not just for myself, not just to look better in myself and feel better myself, which is a part of it.

But also I have a duty. I have a responsibility to the people who I'm around. The world isn't all sunshine and rainbows as Rocky once quoted. And you know that once in a while, me and you once a year, once every year and a half, will be in a situation where I have never been rattled. I've never turned and fled on you. I've always toed the line and rolled with the punches every single time. It's my duty to you as my brother, because who else are you going to walk beside. You want to walk beside some fat loser brother with a little bit of extra money who can't throw a punch?

Well, that's well and good when the drinks are coming in every weekend. But that one situation, it's the difference between life and death. It really is. The places we go, the things we've been through, it really fucking is.

So you were 100%, right. I now concede this thirteen years later. You are completely right. And that is the last argument me and you have ever had. The last serious argument.

ANDREW

Yeah, that's true. It's official. And it's true that people have no duty to themselves. The reason they don't feel that duty to the people around them, is cause they have no duty to themselves. The reason I can command such respect from my females is because if shit goes down, I'm prepared to defend them. Most men aren't prepared to defend them. If you come and try to damage my girl in front of me, even if there is three of you, someone's getting hit. I don't give a fuck.

So because I'm in that position, I also get to be the guy who says" get me coffee, dinner, and get my shit..." It has to be reciprocated. People don't want to put themselves in that position of authority because with authority comes responsibility. So they avoid the responsibilities. But then they get upset they don't have authority. I see all these skinny dickheads on Twitter. Little fucking dorks saying "Women should listen to men! Women should listen to men!" Why the fuck would she listen to you? You can't even do 20 pushups. Fucking no one's gonna listen to you.

No chick's gonna look at you and go, "I need to worship this man". Is she fuck?! And this is why all these fucking liberal dorks and all these little weak, geek guys are saying, "Well, women should listen to men anyway". Well, they say that because no woman listens to them. They want to feel better about the whole situation.

Tristan

Yeah, they want to poison the minds of women.

ANDREW

They're idiots. And when people have no personal responsibility, they don't have any responsibilities to people around them. I know being around me affords personal security. And in return, if you're a female, I want see some titties. Pretty fair trade.

Tristan

And we have friends. I have to say we have friends who aren't as highly trained as us. They don't take it perhaps as seriously as us, but we don't hang around on a serious note with any person who isn't ready to toe the line if punches start flying. You know, if I'm out with five dudes and I'm buying bottles in the club, and I've invited people here to hang out with me, and shit hits the fan. If they're not ready to throw a single punch, you can't hang out with that type of person.

Keep in mind, I'm 6ft 4, 107 kg. I'm the guy that no one starts on unless we're outnumbered. Me and Andrew have never been a fair fight. We're out numbered every single time. Now I could be 120 kg if I were the type of guy to take anabolic steroids and pump all these heavy weights and shit. I'm big enough. And believe me, you don't want me to hit you. For all those people who hate on Andrew out in the world in fact, this is a warning. I am walking next to him and you don't want me to hit you. 110 kilos is what? 250lbs. I'm a quarter of an Imperial tonne and I will knock you the fuck out. So yeah, you're right. I'm glad I've been training ever since that short break, and I've won a British title since and become a well enough accomplished professional fighter. But also on the street, I'll fucking hurt someone.

ANDREW

You have to. That's the rule of the street.

Right I got some questions here. What if you both like the same girl? And that question shows how people don't understand our relationship. As if a female could ever come along, and for a little bit of pussy, mean you were gonna even 1% argue.

Tristan

The person who asked that question, when he finds a girl

he wants to fuck. He likes her. I don't like any woman. I fuck plenty of women. I don't like them. It'll never be "Oh, I like them so much. Oh, my brother likes her too". As if some female is so fucking smart and so beautiful and so mesmerising, that she has captured for the first time ever, my admiration and my brother at the same time. Impossible situation.

It just doesn't happen. The moment Andrew goes on a date with a girl, the moment he's texting a girl or a girl hits me up on Instagram, I say look at this chick. And if he says "oh, I've been messaging her", she's deleted. The interest level legitimately drops to zero. It's not. "Ah, he got there first. Oh, I'm so upset".

Andrew

There's 3.6 billion chicks. Yeah, and you have one brother. You gonna fucking argue over a bimbo? What the fuck is wrong with people? That question even being asked annoys me.

People don't get it, all the things we just talked about being combat ready and shit. As if I'm gonna stop talking to you and I'm gonna start walking around with this bimbo instead. I'm gonna get jumped. She's gonna do nothing but scream.

Tristan

Now there is a hypothetical situation that has never, ever happened. But let's just continue down this path of crazy craziness. One of my main chicks or one of your main chicks. We've been with each of them three, four, five years, depending on the girl. Cool. If one of Andrew's chicks or one of my chicks messaged the other brother in any way that seems like in advance... In fact, we haven't even spoken about this so I'm going to do the conversation... "Yo, Andrew, your main girl, that blonde one's been messaging me, and she's made it very clear she wants to fuck.

. . .

ANDREW

I'll dump her then.

Tristan

All right, I block her, he blocks her. She's gone. No one's getting in between this. You're fucking out your mind.

ANDREW

People don't get it. Just like not even close, there is not an option.

Tristan

Dumb question.

ANDREW

Why do we share bank accounts?

Tristan

Well, I mean, we share... All the money used to be in your bank account. You ran into some troubles. Now all the money is in my bank account. Why do we share bank accounts? We don't have to share bank accounts, but it just makes things easier. The way I run things I'm not going to explain to anyone besides, maybe if the war room guys ask me a question, then I guess I'll explain it in further detail. But the things we own, we own together until the other one dies.

So technically, the Lamborghini is in your name, technically this house is in the name of a company that I own solo. It doesn't matter. So why do we share bank accounts? Because it doesn't matter. We both have cards to all the banks that we have. That's why. And there's no possibility ever that one of us is going to take the money and ignore the other brother. Like, it just wouldn't happen.

ANDREW

Agree. Right. Who has more girls? You're the handsome one.

Tristan

Yeah. You know, I will actually say in terms of quantity of women in our let's say, current roster, typically the number... I will have a higher number.

ANDREW

We've actually had comments from people who come to visit us in Romania, saying that they know professional athletes that don't have a roster of the size and quality of yours. There's been times you've had, like, seven famous Instagram models at a time. Plus six or seven others, plus your girlfriends. Ridiculous.

Tristan

See, I think the main reason is this. One, you're a sniper. You like to focus on a target, and that woman will be more in love with you. Okay. I got one or two main chicks who are super in love with me, but on average, you'll keep five girls who would take a bullet for you. I have my one or two that would do that.

But I'm not a sniper. You see, I'm a fucking flame thrower. I want all of them. I'm a collector. There's nothing else for me to do at this point in my life.

Me and you together have got to a point where we work 10 hours a week. That's it. And I have the money. I have the fucking influence. I have the charm to get as many women as I want. That's my hobby. That's what I like to do. So yeah, a lot of my girls who I'm banging are random hoes, girls from the strip club. That's cool. But in terms of number, my roster is certainly bigger. But in terms of devotion, which is actually the real currency... If you know anything about women, if you watch the PhD course, the devotion to a man, you've got more devoted loyal girls.

ANDREW

Yeah, I've got more girls who like crying their eyes out when I go on holiday.

Tristan

But I got hoes.

ANDREW

Yeah, you got hoes. When I say i'm going away for a week, they all start crying because the idea of me being away for a week damages their brains.

Tristan

Yeah, I'm on vacation with one or two angry text messages, finding new hoes.

. . .

ANDREW

Where all mine are "I can't live without you". It's hard be a Tate. It ain't easy.

Right next. Who would win in a fight?

Tristan

Right. Nonsensical question. Because we never fight.

If you were to bring it down to one person has to knock out the other person? We're so trusting of each other that anyone can win. I punch you in the back of the head, you punch me in the back of the head, something nonsense. In a kick boxing fight, you kick my ass every time.

In a kick boxing match, you win every time. You are the best kickboxer in the world. And when people say this to me, they say, "Oh, your brother would beat you at kickboxing".

You know my replies? "My brother would beat YOU at kick boxing too. He's the world champion". If your brother was Muhammad Ali, would you be upset that he can outbox you? Or you would you be like, "Yeah, my brother's the fucking man". And that's the guy I got by my side. So you are the better kickboxer absolutely.

I'd say in a street fight because it's unfair and I could get a slip on you. I've got two out of ten. Two fights out of ten I can maybe hit you and get the better of you.

Maybe. Yeah I'm heavier, bigger. It would have to be some weird scenario. But you are the better fighter. You are the best fighter in the world. I'll just say for the people at home that think I'm conceding to not being able to fight, I will whoop your fucking ass. Like this guy's the best in the world, quite literally. And he's my bodyguard. So if you start on me, he's going to beat you up too.

. . .

ANDREW

So when did we first start living together? Tell the story. When we first moved in, how broke we were. What job did we even have? We first moved into Frederick's Gate. You were already living outside the family house. You moved out before me. When did we first move in together? I can't remember, 17 or something.

Tristan

Yeah, about 17. No, I just turned 18. I moved out of Mum's house because I couldn't stand living there. I was trying to get my dick sucked and shit. You can't be living with your Mum.

I lived in a big shared house and all of my housemates were various students and people who worked at the airport with me. I worked a very low level job and I was paying, like, £200 a week for rent. And you would start making some money selling television advertising campaigns. You were getting some relatively large commission cheques.

I had some money saved up and we decided to rent an apartment together. We picked the best apartment in Luton, which for two people, 18 and 19 was very expensive. We wasted all of our saved money on that one old Porsche Boxster that you had. We were flat broke every month. It was a struggle to pay the rent. We had some fun, though. We had some parties.

ANDREW

Yeah, we had the best apartment. We had the Porsche, we were cruising around the fucking club, picking up hoes. It was like party house. It's like fucking Geordie Shore shit going on. But we were flat broke.

. . .

Tristan

Yeah, but I saw some bullshit on Facebook recently where someone was like, "Well, I was gonna buy a car for 200 grand some years ago, but my wife convinced me to buy an apartment block and now it's worth 650. I love her". And I started switching on these people like, money isn't the only measurement of success. And people think that me and you think money is the only measurement of success. It is not. How fun your life is is the measurement of success. But if you have fun playing video games and smoking weed you're still a dork.

For example, I know girls, who are air stewardesses, they fly to different countries all the time. They hang out for three or four days. They take their photos at the five star hotels and, to me they're successful people. They're living the dream, you know. So we spunked all our money on this fucking apartment and this one car that we fucking used to drive around in. We had almost zero bank balances. Every time we did get money, we'd go out and get drunk, get pissed.

But look at the memories we have now, 13 years later. I could own another apartment in Luton, slaving away at work and sleeping every night and jerking off. But that's not the way to live life. And the memories me and you have from that time are fucking amazing.

ANDREW

It's true. The fat dream.

Tristan

Don't remind me. That's a story. That's a story for the war room.

.   .   .

ANDREW

Alright, the war room is going to have a story about the fat dream.

Tristan

Guys in the war room ask me the story of the fat dream and I'm going to send you a voice note detailing the story. But that's not for public consumption. That's not civilian shit.

ANDREW

You can tell the story of the watch. We bought the watch. You bought that around the same time.

Tristan

So we were completely flat broke. I'll start from the beginning. People ask me today why I wear a watch that's worth no more than maybe a grand if I tried to sell it second hand. Brand new, you could buy something equivalent for about two and a half. It's a Versace watch gold plated. I don't have a Rolex. I don't have a Hublot. I don't actually own another watch. This watch doesn't even tell the time it is broken. It has been 20 minutes past eleven for the last God knows how long. It's the middle of the afternoon here.

I wear this watch because it is a reminder of the indomitable spirit of man. My brother went to Slovakia. Well, we were both in Slovakia. I came home one day before because my holiday pay had run out and I had to go to work. So he calls me and said, "Something amazing happened. I won some money in the casino". I'm like, "Really? How much?" He said €5000. I'm like, "Fucking good. We need to pay the rent. We got these payments to make on the car insurance. And we need the money. Good. Take the 5000 Euro. Don't go back to the casino".

He comes home. I said, "Where's the cash?" he goes "I don't have any cash. I bought this watch". This watch cost what back then? This is what, 10, 11 years ago, probably 4000 something euros. He'd spent it all on this fucking watch. And it wasn't an argument as such. But I was pissed. You know, I'm like, we need to pay the rent. We need to pay this. How can you just spend it on a watch? What's that what's going to do for you? And you said to me, "We'll make more money. Don't worry. We'll make more money". So we had our little argument and got on with life. And I completely forgot about that small falling out until it's about six years ago now, I was 24. You were 25. And we had indeed made more money. And we were walking through West-field Shopping Centre.

And you bought your Hublot watch. You saw it for sale. It was 12,900 British pounds. And you said, "I like that watch". I said, "okay, go get the watch". You walk through the shop, use the card, you get the watch, and then you take this one off and you give it to me. And you said, "Tristan, do you remember when I said, we'd make more money?" And I was like, "you motherfucker". We did.

ANDREW

I was right. Yeah. At the time, we had no money and then we were buying watches.

Tristan

So this is a reminder of Andrew's unshakable self confidence in himself and a reminder to myself to remember that I am one of the Tate brothers. I'm not the guy who's going to be crying about, oh, we can't pay our bills, this and that. No, I'll make more money. If there's something I want, I'll make more. And that has been my attitude ever since that argument, in fact. But I wear this watch as a reminder. That's why I don't take this off. And that's why I don't have a Rolex.

And that's why when I hang around people who are very rich and have very nice watches, they ask, "why are you wearing just a Versace watch but you drive a quarter of million pound car?" Because I like this watch. That's why.

ANDREW

Yeah, motherfucker, I like this watch. And we did make more money. And that's the reality. You gotta believe. The thing is, with money, especially. I talk about money to people all the time. Me and you have never, ever been savers or penny pinchers. We had $10 and we are in the bar. The round is gonna cost $9.99 and we've walked home. We have been flat broke. When I say flat, broke, I don't mean like we're a little bit poor and we have to go into our savings. I never had savings.

Tristan
    Never.

ANDREW
    No, we've never had.

Tristan
    Not for four or five years ago. But now we only have savings because we do everything we want. But we earn enough that it just piles up.

                           .   .   .

ANDREW

Yeah it's accidental savings. We've never been savers. We've never been penny pinchers ever. We used to spunk all our money. We could scrape together £25, go in the bar, spend it all trying to get laid and trying to pick some chicks up. We've never been savers. And the reality is, the reason I've never been a saver is because you cannot save yourself rich. If you're earning 2000 a month and you want to start saving money to get rich, how the fuck's that gonna work?

You're never. Even if you managed to go to work every day. You walk to work and you stop eating food, and you live outside and you're homeless. You have no rent, no bills, no food. And you save your 2000 a month and you save every single paycheck. You're still not going to be able to afford a Lambo for like 15 years. So how the fuck? Me and you got a Lambo, Bentley, an Aston, a Range Rover, an X6. You're going to work your whole life and not even get our cars. Let alone our houses or our lifestyle. So you can't save yourself rich. So what's the fucking point in saving?

Tristan

And the decision to spend money on this watch didn't prevent me from having the Aston Martin. It's not like you were gonna have the money anyway. Give it another month and the money would have been gone. We would have gone out to clubs and drank it away or done something crazy with it. So saving is the wrong mindset. Don't worry about saving. Worry about making yourself more money.

ANDREW

Yeah, you have to make more money if you ever want to get

rich. There's no such thing as saving yourself rich. That's some bullshit. That's some garbage.

Right. You're the younger brother. If you had a younger brother, what would you teach him?

Tristan

Jesus, if I had a younger brother, what would I teach him? You know, I teach them the same things Dad taught us. It was that simple. I mean, I appreciate everything you've always done for me. But you were just really passing the torch down from our Dad, who was the man.

Basically, every lesson you have in life and every lesson you learn in life from a real man was from him. And some of them didn't quite reach me. I was a few years younger and you had to pass them down to me. That's fine. It would be exactly the same thing. Passing the torch. I'd make him train. I'd make him combat ready. I'd make him learn how to fight. I make him know the importance of not letting women get a hold of your brain.

I teach him the importance of everything, self restraint, knowledge, reading all the shit that we do, playing chess. He'd do all of it.

Andrew

Women getting hold on your brain. Let's talk about that for minute. Why do you think, it's the number one problem? Why do you think men are becoming such bitches for chicks? Why do you think chicks are starting to rule the world? Why are women taking control of men as a whole? What's happened to men saying to women "You know what? Shut up". Where is that going?

. . .

Tristan

Well, a lot of this, actually, you cover this in your PhD course. But it's a simple matter that's happened to the world. With the internet and social media and everything coming along, women no longer value the attention of men. I was furious a couple years ago when that ugly bitch walked through New York City, and counted all the times she was "cat-called", and she said,"We need to end street harassment".

Look, you can't go up and touch a woman. You can't go up and grab a woman.

I agree that's assault. But there is nothing wrong with seeing an attractive woman and walking up and trying to make an honest approach to have sex with them. That's how that bitch's parents met. That's how that bitch's grandparents met. Her great great great grandfather saw her great great great grand-mother and thought, you know what? I like her. "Hi. What's your name?" He didn't think about starting a family. He thought about fucking.

Now, male attention is so prevalent, it's everywhere. Girls have Instagram pages. Patreons. They're collecting money, Patreon for doing nothing.

They're collecting money for being themselves and talking shit and posting pictures. And men are handing their money over. If I were a girl i'd do the same. I'm not mad at them, but the world is fucked. You're completely right. And women could get hold of a man's brain because an average girl can make herself so in demand via the power of the Internet, etc. that when one guy's with her, he's like, "Well, I'm lucky to have her. She's actually really special", but they don't really believe it. They're just repeating the words that she's putting in his mind, if you know what I mean. So that can happen to a young man.

When I was 18, 19, I've had some girlfriends that I was perhaps way too interested in, who I look back and I think they were just uninteresting bitches, but I was young. I was getting my dick sucked by an eight for the first time. I thought, "Wow, she's special". Now that I'm a fully aware, established man, Jesus Christ! I'm lucky I didn't fall down the trap of getting those hoes pregnant and marrying her.

My life would suck. So no, I would stop my little brother from doing that. I guess this question can be rephrased as to how will I raise my sons. Because that will happen. I will not have a younger brother, but I will have sons.

ANDREW

Last question. People want to know how we started out, those who don't know. We made most of our money with a webcam company. So people want to know. I've talked about it a lot, and it's more your interview. Tell the entire story of how we started a webcam company. How did it come about? And for all the people who are still interested in starting a webcam company - first, you need the PhD course because you think you know about girls but you don't. But I have 22 girls with my name tattooed on them.

You don't have any because you don't know shit about girls. First you need to get that. Then you can get the webcam course where me and Tristan are teaching you how to own a webcam company from the ground up.

But tell the whole story of how we ended up starting a webcam company and actually officially becoming millionaires instead of just pretending to be, in our fucked-up Porsche and our apartment.

Tristan

Yeah, well, the problem that we always had in life is that we were always good with women. I don't give a shit what people say, but I hear all the time "Oh girls like you because you have money". Do you know how many girlfriends I've had when I was broke? I slept on a mattress on the floor for a year in one bedroom of an apartment that I shared. And that mattress saw more action than most fucking dudes will their whole life.

Andrew

I verify this is true. Me and Tristan and another guy were sharing an apartment. We had no living room. We turned a living room to a bedroom and we were all sharing. And Tristan's bed frame broke when smashing some chick. And I said, "You're gonna buy a new bed frame?" He said "No, they're too expensive". So he put his mattress on the floor and carried on smashing chicks.

Tristan

In fact, back in the day, and if the War Room ask her name, I'm going to tell her name to the War Room, but one girl was a very successful glamour model from the UK who was on one of those Babestation channels at the time. And this was eight years ago. I don't know what she's up to these days, but she was one of the Babestation chicks. She was well known. She was at parties in London, and she got smashed on my mattress, on the floor.

So I've always been good with women. Fuck money. Women don't chase me for money. I've always been good. Now we had this problem where we've always had so many beautiful women. But women were something you had to spend money on. And we knew there was a better system to that. Now you take a girl out for dinner, you take a girl out for lunch, and you go back to your job to get more money to repeat the cycle. You in fact, Andrew, you cracked the code.

So I was working a job at the time. It was a sales job where I was selling some bullshit kind of home improvement. It was something quite unique. I was making good money because I'm good at sales. I'm good at various things, and I'm not afraid of hard work. I was making about one to one and a half thousand British pounds every week, which is more than 90% of people make. So I was doing very well.

But I was working seven days a week. So I asked Andrew if he wanted a job doing the same thing. And Andrew said "No, because if I go to work and do that, then that's who we're going to be. I need my time and my space to work out how to do different shit". So I was paying the car insurance. I was paying the rent. All the money was coming in from me at that time. Andrew's net income was £0, but he was thinking. Which is very important.

This is why you've got to take your time to think. After your nine to five. At 6pm, you get home, don't switch on the TV. Think of your way out. And I gave Andrew the space to think.

So he realised that he had so many beautiful girlfriends. I think he got one of them a job on a Babestation channel. And she came home one day blabbering some nonsense that Andrew is half-listening to. Saying "Yeah, some of these girls make money on webcam". Now to me and Andrew, we thought "Who pays for webcams?"

I mean, porn is free. Who pays for webcams? That's got to be a dying industry because me and Andrew aren't fucking cucks, and we don't go on webcam, and we don't pay women for their time and attention. So we never even considered it as a viable financial option.

Andrew sat down. He worked it all out. Not just how to put her on webcam, but how to maximise the amount of money this one girl was making. And I came home from work one day. And what words did you say?

· · ·

ANDREW

I said "Something amazing has happened".

Tristan

Something amazing has happened. I said, "Yeah, what?" He said "I've made £350 today". So I was like, I made 250. What the fuck's going on here? How did you make £350? And he shows me this number on the screen next to one of his girls videos broadcasting. He said "That's money that's going to come to my bank account". Now, I'd never seen money on a screen unless it was like an online casino. So I was like, "Do you have to gamble it?" And he says, "No, that's real earned money on its way to my bank account."

So rather than me going out slaving all day, I had a few chicks of my own. I put one on webcam in my apartment. Then we had four girls on cam in two bedrooms, one after the other. I slept in the hall. I was that money hungry.

And from there we upgraded to a four bedroom, five bedroom penthouse over in Hertfordshire. Then we left the fucking UK because it's shit. In Romania you have faster Internet, more girls, prettier girls. And we just grew into an empire.

We were making $2 million a year from Webcam alone. It's that big of an industry, but you have to be man enough to scale it up. And we also worked out the best ways of doing it, and the best way of monetising girls.

So, yeah, that was really the time when we stopped being pretenders. Because at the time, I had a Range Rover that was paid for. I did own it outright, but it had 100,000 miles on it. It was getting a little bit old, and I had no means of upgrading or replacing it.

That's how we made our first legitimate million US dollars. And we had a million in the bank account. And we fucking partied that week.

. . .

ANDREW

People will attack us say, girls only like you for money, and they don't understand that we only have money because we had girls. I mean, I was making money fighting. But by the time you get paid... I mean, I was world champion, but it's kickboxing. It's not boxing.

So if I am gonna get paid 20 grand for a fight, 20% for your manager, 30% tax, all this bullshit driving to the gym back and forth every day. It's fuck-all to live on, it's nothing. So people are like, "Oh, you only have girls because you have money". We only started making money because we had so many chicks around the house.

And you're right. I said to you "If I come and join your sales job, then who we are is salesmen, we're windows salesman. We got nice cars. We make money. But then we're both windows salesman". So you had to pay the bills. I needed to sit there and think. And for two months, you worked every day. We never argued. You never complained that I didn't contribute, and you went out to work every morning while I sat on my ass thinking of a way to make us some fucking money.

Tristan

Yeah, yeah.

ANDREW

And that's what happened. I end up flying in some chick and putting her on babe station, blah blah, ended up with this whole webcam company.

"Something amazing has happened". I remember because I came into your room and I said it, and you were with your girlfriend at the time. After we discussed about the money on the screen, you said to your girlfriend 'Well you can do cam." and she goes, "I don't want to do it.".

Tristan
What happened to her?

ANDREW
You dumped her the next day. The next day, you said, "Well, someone's gonna work because I'm going to work every day. Andrew's at home making more money than me. So I want a girl on cam and if it ain't gonna be you it's gonna be someone else". And she got fresh to you over the phone. I remember you hung up on her and called up another girl and said, "Come over, we're gonna make some money."

Tristan
Yep. She was one of my best earners. I kept her for about two years. She was good.

ANDREW
But the first girl who got fresh, I never saw her again. And you were with her like a year and a half!

Tristan
Every girl who got fresh you never saw her again. It's the way me and you work. Every girl gets fresh today, you never see them again.

· · ·

ANDREW

True. And if your chick is ride or die, really loves you, what's the problem getting a bunch of money from home? What's the issue? Oh, they gonna see your titties. Your titties are basically out on Instagram for free anyway.

Tristan

So that's the question. That's a question to all you guys at home. You know, if you're interested in making a lot of money, this is how me and Andrew did it. I was actually kind of resenting the fact that he was selling our knowledge, et cetera. But me and Andrew are scaling down the webcam operation. We're into some other things now that are making us a lot of money. So by all means, Andrew go and sell the information.

But all you guys at home consider if you were down and out, would your girl make money to help you? Because honestly, if your girl won't wave her titties at a computer, if that girl won't do it for you to help change both of your lives, get rid of her straight away because she ain't ever gonna help you do shit.

ANDREW

It's true. Like, oh, morals. Oh, blah, blah. I mean, a lot of girls have confidence issues. They don't wanna do it because they're self conscious and stuff. But you're right, man. If you're saying to your chick "Look, we're together forever. I'm gonna change our lives, we're gonna become millionaires. All you got to do is sit here in a bra". What the fuck is the problem? I mean, since we've been doing this job five years now, how many girls worked for us? Seventy five? A hundred? So many girls. How many of them worked for us and didn't sleep with one of us?

. . .

Tristan

One.

ANDREW

Who's that one?

Tristan

The girl from Lithuania. She sucked your dick.

ANDREW

Yeah, she escaped, I guess.

Tristan

But she worked for us for a very short time.

ANDREW

It was like a week. But the all the others slept with one of us at some point. We've been through a shit load of chicks. The most loyal survive, that's how it is.

Tristan

And I've got my most loyal girls even still, I've had them years. One of them is retired from work for me. She's pursuing other things and I've kept her. You know why? Because when the chips were down, when I needed money, when I needed to build my empire, she was there fucking rubbing her tits for losers on camera and collecting the fucking money.

. . .

ANDREW

There's no secret to all how we made our money gentlemen, that's how we did it. We were internet pimps and now we're no longer in the industry. We used to have, like, 30, 40 girls online. Now we're much smaller. We got a couple left who just have regular fans. We're moving into other things. We've got some property deals and stuff in Eastern Europe. And that's why we're now teaching you guys how to do it.

So anyone who's interested in Webcamming or PhD, or any of those things. Wanna learn how to get girls, I teach you. If you wanna learn how to run a webcam studio, you buy the course.

You get direct access to me. Tristan will Skype with you any time you want. And we'll teach you exactly how to do it.

And then maybe one day you'll be in a penthouse with ten naked chicks and a Lamborghini outside. And you'll think those Tate brothers are pretty fucking smart because we are.

~

WHY YOU'LL NEVER BE RICH

On the 12th of March of this year, something amazing happened.

Due to all the Corona virus lockdowns and blah de blah, everyone started panicking and getting locked in their houses. Then the price of Bitcoin plummeted 50% in like 2 hours. Nobody really remembers that.

I remember.

And on the 12th March, I put a tweet on my Twitter account saying "You're all pussies. We all know it's gonna come back. Buy as much as you can. I'm about to buy a bunch".

Of course a lot of people start replying under it. "Actually no, this is the end of Bitcoin and the monetary system".

People do not seem to yet understand that crisis and opportunity are the same thing. In fact, in Japanese they have the same word.

And what most of you people are doing is you're going through your life and you're seeing a crisis, or thinking you're seeing the world get destroyed. You're seeing Corona, you're seeing the American election be stolen.

You're seeing all these bad things happen, and you do not

identify any opportunity in these circumstances. You sit there and think, "Oh, well, dum du dum, the world does what it does and I'll keep doing my job working at Starbucks and maybe one day when my ship comes in, I'll make some money".

Never. That's never going to happen. It's never going to happen. And I'm gonna tell you why.

THREE REASONS most of you are never going to be rich.

One, you do not identify opportunity. The opportunity we're discussing now, which happened on the 12th of March where I bought 600 grand of Bitcoin, which is now worth an excess of 7 million.

I've done zero work.

Zero.

I've turned 600k into 7 million. Just because I identified an opportunity that took me ten minutes. That's how easy it is.

NOW YOU PROBABLY DIDN'T HAVE 600K to buy Bitcoin like I did. Fine. But you could still have made huge profits with the amount you do have. The problem is, you do not identify opportunities.

This is the first thing you not do. You do not pay attention to the world around you. You just live in your little bubble. You're too busy arguing with your ugly girlfriend. Too busy stressed out about some dumb shit. Too busy sleeping in. You don't pay attention. You're not perspicacious. This is why you miss opportunities. The first reason you're never going to be rich.

SECOND REASON you're never going to be rich, is that everything that is taught and told about wealth creation is outdated. Your parent's idea of how to generate wealth no longer works. Your parents say just work hard, save your money, put it in a savings account and then get a mortgage, and then you can pay off the house.

All garbage.

That stuff doesn't work anymore. Back when your parents were doing that, the savings account gave them 7% interest. Now you don't even get 1%.

Pay off the house?! How much cheaper was a house in relation to their wages than than it is now? It's insane.

If you actually try and make money just by putting it in a savings account, getting a mortgage and paying off the mortgage, you're going to be broke until you're sixty. That's not getting rich. You need to be rich when you're young and sexy like me, not when you're old. Because nobody cares about the old dude in the Lambo. They care about the young dude in the Lambo.

So everything you've been told and taught about wealth creation is outdated and wrong. Everything has changed. The whole game has changed, and I even say to people all the time, the ones I mentor and coach, don't buy a house, rent a house.

They ask "But isn't that wasting money?"

No.

What's wasting money is buying a house, giving huge interest rates to a fucking bank and then tying yourself to one geographical location. The reason humans are the number one species on the planet is because of our adaptability. I can go anywhere on Earth. I can go wherever the money is. Where the money resides.

If the money is residing in Japan, I can go to Japan. If I need to go to Singapore, I can go to Singapore. I can live in Las motherfucking Vegas. Wherever I'm gonna get paid, I can go and I'll just rent. rent, rent, rent, boom, boom boom.

I ain't got nothing tying me down. It ain't going gonna take years for me to buy or sell something. I ain't gonna worry about all the upkeep and property maintenance. Buying a house is foolish.

I do own my Bucharest house because I wanted it to be exactly the way I like it. But I'm *rich* rich, right? You aren't.

So you shouldn't be doing that shit anyway.

You do not need to buy a house. It's one of the biggest mistakes you can make. It's a psychological thing that your parents have told you. And I tell people this and they go, "Oh yeah, but you can always rent it out".

You're going to spend 300,000 on a house so that you can rent it out for 800 a month?

And then every time the boiler breaks, you're going to spend 500 fixing the boiler, and they're gonna damage your house. There's gonna be a whole bunch of repairs. They are calling all the time with hassle and stress, and that's if they even pay the rent on time. Do you think that's a good spend of 300 grand? Do you know what else you can do with 300 grand?

Buy Bitcoin.

Revolutionary. Your real estate can be on the blockchain instead of out here, because when it's on the blockchain, it can be sold instantly. You ever tried to sell a house? It takes years. Ever try to sell Bitcoin? It takes seconds.

So this is the second reason you're never going to be rich. Because all your ideas and concepts of how wealth is graded are outdated.

THREE. The third and most important reason you're never going to be rich is because you do not have a plan. You do not have a plan to get rich. Nothing good has ever happened on accident. Have you ever met a guy who just got covered in muscles and a six pack? You're like, "hey, bro, how did you do that? You been to the gym?" "No, man it was just an accident".

Of course not. He built that body purposefully. He did

things specifically to get the result he desired. He ate a specific way. He trained a specific amount. He knew exactly what he was doing.

Every rich person knows exactly what they're doing. People who are making money know exactly how to do it. You're sitting there saying I want to be rich. You don't even have a plan to get rich. How the fuck are you going to get rich on accident? How's that gonna happen? Oops, I'm a millionaire. Never.

So one, you do not pay attention to opportunities and crisis.

Two, everything you understand about wealth creation is outdated and wrong.

And three, you do not have a plan. Here's where I come in. Because I have a plan for you.

So WE TALKED about my little Bitcoin story.

I made 7 million.

I'm the man, we all know I'm the man. That's why you're reading my book.

But there's something new in the world now called decentralized finance. I don't know if you're familiar with that.

I'm not particularly familiar with it. I'm certainly not a technical dork. I don't completely understand it, but I have very smart people who work for me who do understand it, because that's what happens when you're the boss. You hire people who know things, right? All those people who went to expensive universities that I didn't go to.

But these dorks who work for me, they know a bunch of shit. And what they're doing is they're getting me a 30 or 40% return on my money. So I'm giving them 100 grand and I'm getting 30-40% a year. The bank doesn't even give 1%.

.   .   .

WE JUST TALKED about how the old ways of wealth generation, like putting it in a savings account are aiming for 6 or 7%.

I can give you 30-40% if you get involved in our centralized finance program. If you want to know more about this, it doesn't matter if you have €5, it doesn't matter if you have €5 million, you can get huge profits on your money with decentralized finance. And I am happy to teach you exactly how.

I'm fixing all three of the problems. I've identified an opportunity within the crisis.

They've turned on the money printers and everything's going to shit. I've identified an opportunity, which is decentralized finance and making huge APRs on my money.

Two, I'm giving you a new way to generate wealth because all of your ideas are outdated. So one I have identified an opportunity. Two, this is a brand new way to generate wealth.

It's already made me $500,000. It's fucking incredible. I'm showing you brand new stuff.

And three, I'm gonna give you a plan. So the three reasons I told you were in your way, I can fix for you.

I have your opportunity. It's brand new and it generates wealth right now today. No outdated ideas. And I give you a plan telling you exactly how to do it. Even if you only have five euro in the bank. I've just fixed your life. What do you say?

Maybe I'm a bit egotistical, some would say, but I'm certainly extremely handsome and intelligent. We can all agree on that.

∽

THE MINDSET YOU MUST HAVE TO
ACHIEVE WHAT YOU WANT

Twitter beef.

I always have a Twitter beef.

I can't be on Twitter for more than 3 seconds without arguing with someone. As soon as I press the button, shit goes down. I am one of those kind of guys. That's why I became so famous on there. I was verified, and they took it away. Came back, took it away from me again. Came back to take it away from me again. It was my fourth fucking account.

Anyway. Now we're gonna talk about the fact that I believe each and every one of you is exactly where you deserve to be in life, or where you belong. Or let me change the wording - You're where you want to be.

So if you're not a millionaire, and you're not happy with your life, guess what? You are where you deserve to be.

And the reason I'm going to say that is as follows: If you claim " Oh I had bad luck this, or I tried this so I can't pull off that blah, blah, blah, blah". You're lying to yourself.

It's impossible to exist somewhere where you're not comfortable. If you were to lay on some red hot stones you'd get up and move because it hurts. It's not comfortable. You have to get out of that position. Yet if you look at your lives, your life is in a shit position, but you still don't move.

You don't do anything about it.

So if it was really, truly uncomfortable to you, like those red hot stones were, you'd change something.

But the fact you refuse to change something shows that you're pretty comfortable where you are. Now of course you can talk a good talk. All you motherfuckers will sit there and go, "Oh, I know my life is not in order. I want to be rich and I want to be in shape, and I want, and I want, and I'm gonna and I'm gonna", and then you don't do anything about it. It only shows that you know how to talk the talk, but you can't walk the walk.

When I was broke, I couldn't sleep. And when I say that people laugh. I'm not joking. I wanted money like I fucking needed air. I am smart enough to know that money equals freedom. And I don't want to live controlled by a job. I don't want to live controlled by a government. I don't want control by anybody. I want to be free. I want to be able to go on Twitter and say what fuck I want, and not worry I'll lose my fucking job.

I NEEDED MONEY. And I used to sit there with my hands on my head and people would ask "What's wrong with you?" I need money. I want money today. I would have been one of those guys that robbed a bank.

If I didn't find money by the time I was 40, I would have walked in there with a fucking shotgun. I'm not gonna live broke. Get rich or die trying. I understand that completely. You mother fuckers are sitting there going "Yeah, I really wanna be a millionaire", and then just going to sleep.

Fuck! You are not uncomfortable enough in your position. Same thing with physical fitness. You're a fat fuck. "Oh, yeah, I really need to lose weight. I know. I'm gonna lose weight". Why are you fat then? Getting fat does not happen quickly. It's a slow process. Didn't you fucking notice across a year? Did you look in the mirror with your eyes closed? You knew what was happening and you were comfortable being fat, because if you weren't comfortable, you would do something about it.

So many people say "Oh my life is fucked up". And I'm like, yeah, of course it is. Because you're happy with your life to be fucked up. Even if you're not happy, even if you're uncomfortable, you're not uncomfortable enough to change it. If you were genuinely unhappy about your position, you would not be coming to me for motivation. If you were genuinely pissed off about your situation, you would not need me to motivate you. You would motivate your fucking self and you would do something to change it yourself.

But you don't.

Which says a lot. So this whole motivational shit, it's all garbage. All you fuckers are exactly where you belong.

I am where I belong. The top of the mountain with a fucking Lambo, Bentley, Aston, mansions, millions in liquid cash, and 20 girlfriends. This is where I fucking belong because I refused to stay anywhere else. And if you motherfuckers are still sleeping soundly at night, you're going to stay exactly where you are.

∾

HOW TO GET RICH

P eople always ask me how to make money. "Give me some tips and tricks to make money".

Well, there's two important factors when it comes to being financially successful. The first one is you motherfuckers need to learn how to control women.

And I realised this from fighting. I saw so many talented fighters go off track when they got a girlfriend, because girls want your time and attention. And you know the saying, time is money. So if you're training full time, five, six hours a day, and then you got to eat properly, you got to rest properly, rehabilitate, etc. You have hardly any time for sitting around.

So when I used to get girls, I was a hit it and quit it guy. When I was training, I didn't have time for this fucking bullshit from women, because I'm fucking training to fight.

I'd fuck her and then I'll be training while she's all "Can I see you today?", "I'm busy", "Can I see you Tuesday?", "I'm busy", "Well fine blah blah!"

Well, then fuck off. I'll go out on Saturday and fuck

someone else. I don't care about you. I'm a fucking professional. If I walk in a bar, I don't leave alone. I'm a G, so I don't fucking play games with these girls.

But when the guys who I'd be training with get a girlfriend, they start having to leave early, or we'd arrange a sparring session on Christmas Day, used to do it every year. And the guy is like "Oh I am with the girlfriend so I can't make it". These are the little things that start to chip away, eat away. And I learned that fighting translates to business. Time is money.

You motherfuckers are out here living a life and you're trying to get paid, and you have a female who's on your fucking case, taking up your time over dumb shit that doesn't put money in the bank.

And the biggest mistake you can make when you're trying to become financially successful, is waste your time. Now when I say, get your female in check, you're all saying it's controversial. But you want to get rich and not waste your time.

If you're arguing with a woman over nothing, then you're just going to a movie you don't want to see. If you're following her around Ikea to choose curtains because she insists you come, or if you're dealing with her bullshit, you're wasting time.

That's money time. You're awake and you could be getting paid, but you're fucking around with some bullshit, with some chick. Worst thing about it is if you got rich, she then wants to spend the money. Imagine you get rich and the whole way up the journey, all she did was fucking complain! So now you're rich, now you want the fucking spoils of it. Did she support you? Did she fuck!

You can get the odd good girls who might do that, but it ain't easy.

And I have good girls, and I've had good girls who supported me. But the only way you find a good girl in the modern world is you fuck 20 first. Thats the reality. And I talked about this in the PhD course on the website. I talk about the test, to see the girl's quality or not. But I only found good girls through trial and error, because we live in a world now where these girls, a lot of them ain't worth shit. Besides the sex. That's all they're worth

And it doesn't matter what kind of man you are. If you get a rotten egg, they're just a pain in the ass. Every 20 girls I fuck, I find a good one. But if you're going out there fucking one or two girls and settle down with her, then you're probably stuck with some basic-ass bitch, who is slowing down your progress.

So when people say to me, how do I get rich? First thing I say is dump your girlfriend. "But Tate why dump her?" Okay, then don't dump her. Tell her that you're going to quit your job because you want to chase your dreams of running your own business.

Tell her that she has to continue to work. Tell her that she's paying the rent, and you're borrowing her car, and you're not going to have a penny for the next two years. And if she doesn't agree to that shit, then dump her. Simple.

That's how you know you've got a quality woman or not? If she's a quality woman she'll say "Okay, I believe in you. Follow your dream. I'll do my best."

Do that. And if she says, "Well, no, why am I working, if you're not working? And what about on the weekend we're supposed to go here, it is my birthday." Then she's just a fucking dick head. You're not gonna get rich with that shit in your ear. You're not gonna do it.

So it depends. What do you want more? Mediocre sex with some fucking bitch, or cash and unlimited hoes when you're at the top of the mountain? I was smart enough to do the right thing. I'd hit it and quit it, when I needed to get laid because I'm a fucking G. I'm a professional. I add next-level dark-triad, fucking black magic skills to get laid. I didn't leave the club alone. It's all in the PhD course. It's all on the fucking website.

. . .

So I understood this when I was fighting from a young age. Every 20 girls I fuck, I find a good one and I keep. So now I'm at the top of the mountain because I stopped the mistakes early on.

People are fucking up their income having to deal with women, and they never get to the point where they get unlimited women. If you do it my way and you get your shit together, then women lose value because you've got so many girls.

Even Christian McQueen, he was here in Romania. I was scrolling through my Instagram showing him the girls hitting me up. He was like, "I've never seen that. I've not even seen that with famous sports stars".

I get nonstop girls trying to fuck me. I don't have time. I wake up, go to the gym, go film some TateSpeech, go for dinner with my bro. Then I want to hang out with guys, cause women annoy me anyway. I'll text a bitch at 11:00 p.m. "Yeah come to this club." Couple of drinks, bang! I'm fucking five girls a week. I got eight fucking girlfriends. It's crazy. And that's because I didn't fuck up at the beginning.

So if you really care about sex that much, and you really need to get laid that much and sit around with girls, then it's still better to do things my way because you're gonna end up with more pussy in the end anyway. Stop fucking around with complaining females. Do not let your woman ruin your life, because you may think she improves your life, but most of the time she's ruining it. She's slowing you down and she's sucking up your fucking time. That's stopping you, getting rich.

Second thing, which is semi related, translates to friends. So all the things I said about the girl taking your time up. That translates to a friend also. If your friends just want to smoke weed and play video games, then you ain't gonna get anywhere. So all those lessons I just discussed, and I don't want to repeat myself, you can also translate over to friends. But on top of that, you need to have soldiers around you on the same mission as you.

If you had a group of soldiers, and some of the soldiers want to attack a position, and some of the soldiers want to defend a position, then you're not a unit. You're doing different things, different objectives.

You need a team on the same mission.

When I sit with my friends, all I talk about is money. Now you may say that's sad. It's not sad because I enjoy money. Yes we talk about other things. We have a laugh. We have a joke. But when successful people sit around the table, they talk about how they're making money. How are you making money? How is he making money? How could you improve making money? What if I helped you make money this way? What if you helped me this way? What if we worked together and made money together?

And this is how money is made. The world is nothing other than people talking. A government is just people in a room talking. The police, people in a room talking. Businesses, people in a room talking. It's just people in a room talking shit and carrying out objectives. The conversations you have are important. When I say this, people go, "Yeah, I agree. I need some rich people to sit and talk to". Well, the reason you don't know anyone who talks that way is because you don't talk about it. If you go sit with your loser friends and only talk about money, and they don't talk about money back, you'll eventually stop talking to them. You won't be friends anymore.

If they go, "Let's play video games". Tell them, "You know what, guys? Video games are shit. We need to get rich. Just talk about how we can get rich".

What's the most money you ever had? Where did you get it from? Who's the richest person you know? If you start talking about that and they go, "Oh, who cares?" and carry on playing the games, then you're not gonna hang around with them anymore. You gonna end up meeting new friends. And by the fucking process of natural selection, like evolution, if you only talk about one thing, you're gonna end up sitting with people who only talk about the same thing. And before you know it, you're gonna have a group of friends around you, and you're all sitting around talking about making fucking money.

And some of you motherfuckers might make some fucking money. It ain't complicated. These are the two most important tips and tricks I can give you when it comes to getting paid. If you want the shortcut you want it easy, like I said, the courses I've made on my fucking website. I'm proud of the shit I did.

I tell you how to control women. Absolutely. How to get women absolutely. I have it all on my website and I tell you exactly how to fucking do it. It doesn't get easier than that.

But even if you buy my courses, if you have a nagging bitch girlfriend and a bunch of loser friends. You're still not going to be half successful as you could be.

∽

THE G MINDSET AND MIND TRICKS

We're going to learn something about ourselves, and learn how you view the world. Because in reality, how you view the world absolutely and utterly shapes how you react to the world, how you act in the world, how people view you. It's all down to how you view things.

THERE'S VERY few things in this life we actually have any control over. I learned all the lessons I'm gonna be talking about the hard way. I didn't learn them in a course. So you guys are very, very lucky. I learned all this shit the absolute hard way

My dad was a straight G. He was in the military and was based in England in the Air Force. My Dad was actually recruited by the CIA and worked for the intelligence services. He was based in England. He met my mom, a pretty little white thing. He was a big black dude.

. . .

So BACK THEN, that was taboo. He grabbed her, took her back to America with him. They had three beautiful off-spring, me being the oldest. And then he continued with his life of being a G, pimping hoes, playing chess at top level, and traveling around Europe.

He never had any large financial sums. He certainly didn't leave me a penny. He didn't have anything to leave. So all he left me with was a mindset, and that mindset was enough that it allowed me to build the life I wanted to build. My father never wanted to be fiscally rich, never gave a shit about being rich. He cared about other things. If he had wanted to be rich, he would have been extremely rich.

I PERSONALLY DECIDED I wanted to be rich. And all of the lessons that I'm gonna be talking about, a lot are from him, and a lot are from experiences of growing up poor, growing up in a single mother household, growing up in social housing or the projects in England.

When my mother and father split, I was nine years old. I became a world level athlete, and now becoming a self-made multimillionaire. So all of these lessons I've learned absolutely the hard way. I can absolutely assure you I know what I'm fucking talking about.

I've lived an extreme life. More extreme than most. Growing up with a single mother, my Mum crying because she can't pay the bills. I went from broke as a joke, to a multi millionaire. I've been a nobody, and I've been famous. I've started from nothing, from the point where I had to run to the gym because I didn't even have a car to get there. I've done it all.

. . .

So MY EXTREME life is where these lessons come from. When I talk about G mindset, G mindset is absolutely the most important thing.

This is actually quite funny. A girl I was dating once, she said to me that I reminded her of Ru Paul. Ru Paul is a famous fucking drag Queen, so I didn't think it was a great comparison. She told me it's because he has a saying:

"I always knew I was famous. I had to wait for the rest of the world to catch up".

And she told me I had the same mindset. She said this to me when I had nothing, because I told everyone I'm gonna be world champion. Years before I even had a British title. Before I even had an English title. I just started fighting. I was like, "I'm the next world champion". I just started saying it with genuine conviction. I knew I would be the best. I genuinely knew I would be the best.

You have to understand in this world everyone constantly tells you to not be arrogant. Do not have an ego. On my Twitter, I put my ego into overdrive because I find it entertaining. But people will constantly tell you to not talk in a way which is full of conviction. People do not like you to have the arrogance and have an ego. They think it's the worst thing ever.

Let me tell you a fact. Number one facet of the G mindset: Your life is never going to be worse if you walk through the world believing you are the fucking man.

You wake up, look in the mirror and go "I'm the fucking man. I am the man". There's no one on this planet who can do shit I couldn't do if I put my mind to it. I don't give a fuck how good you are at piano because if I decide to play piano, I would be better than you at piano. And I believe that. I don't just say these things, I fucking believe them. And when you go through life believing you really, really are the man. There are very few downsides. The downsides are everyone is going to call you arrogant. Everyone calls you dick head. They are gonna say you have a big ego. You're going to lose a few loser friends. Who cares?

What you are going to gain is other people on the same path. You're gonna gain other people who think "Well, I'm the fucking man too. This guy's, the man, let's make some money".

That's what's going to happen. So the first thing you need for a G mindset is you need to start believing that you are the fucking man.

Even if you're not the man yet. Even before I was a world champion, I knew I was gonna be the man. So I don't give a fuck. And I was happy to say that to anybody. When people called me arrogant, stupid and deluded. I just sat there and looked at them and say, "Fuck you, I'm gonna be the man". And this is how, now when my life's kind of come full circle.

I'LL TELL you a very quick story. When I was 21, I had a sales job and I had to drive down to a sales meeting to try and sell some advertising. I had a really old shitty car. And I'm driving my car which I couldn't afford to have fixed. There was a dent in the front, it was all fucking caved in. So I had to park it away from the sales meeting, then walk the rest of the way. So I'm driving this car, and pulling up next to me at the traffic lights, on a fucking Tuesday morning, 10 am with music blasting, in a drop top Aston Martin with a Swedish number plate, is some fucking dude, about 30 with a hot blonde next to him.

And I remember looking at him and thinking, "Who the fuck is this guy?" Here I am with my broken car on my way to fucking do a shit job. I can't afford to fix my car.

This guy is from fucking Sweden and he's just driven to England. He's got this hot bitch, and he's got music pumping, and he's on his way to have lunch. Like, where the fuck did my life go wrong? I wanna be like that guy.

And I think this every single time when I drive around Romania in my fucking Lamborghini, or my Aston Martin, or my Ferrari, or my Bentley, whichever one I decide to drive. And my cars all have English number plates. And I always have a girl with me. And people look at me and are giving me the exact same look I gave that guy. People look at me like "Who the fuck is that guy from England?" They're standing at the bus stop about to go to work, and this guy's got a quarter of a million dollar car and a hot bitch on his way to have lunch with music blaring.

And the reason I managed to go full circle is having those small events in my life like seeing someone who else was more successful than me, ingrained in my brain. And for a lot of people, it doesn't ingrain in their brain.

I WAS WALKING to school once, walking to college with my friends. I went to a college on the other side of town, so I had to walk four fucking miles to college, it was a fucking nightmare. So I had to walk, walk, walk, and halfway I meet some other people so there's a group of five or six of us along the way. And one day a Ferrari passed us and everyone else was like, "Oh yeah, a Ferrari".

I was only 18 and I remember saying to the group, "Doesn't it annoy you that this guy has a fucking £300,000 car, and we'll probably never have one?". And they're like, "Oh, yeah, it's only a car."

They didn't understand. There is a life hack. There's something happening where people are living lives that other people don't get to live. There's something happening. There's something going on. I want to have a £300.000 car. I wanted it and no one else did.

These little events didn't ingrain in their brain. This Ferrari driving past me bothered me, and it bothered me to my core to the point where I decided I would do anything it takes to have one. Whereas other people just saw it and carried on with their normal lives. This is the reason I have six or seven supercars, and other people don't. Because these small events ingrained in my brain. So this is the second thing.

G mindset. First thing you have to believe you're the fucking man, you can achieve anything.

I'm gonna say that again. You have to believe you're the fucking man, and you have to believe you can achieve anything. I'm not saying you can achieve anything easily. I'm not saying it's not gonna take a whole bunch of work. I'm not saying it's going to happen quickly, but you have to believe you can achieve anything.

I'LL TELL you something now. I don't give a fuck about being an astronaut, and I don't care about climbing Mount Everest. But if you give me enough time to train. I will get it done.

I know that for a fact, because I know who I am as a man. That's the first thing.

The second thing is you need to be perspicacious. You need to understand that in this world, there's a whole bunch of people doing amazing shit that you are not doing, and that needs to piss you off. Because when it pisses you off, you become motivated all of a sudden.

I was the only one who was pissed off when that Aston Martin was next to me and I had my sales job. I was the only one who was pissed off when I saw that Ferrari drive past. Other people were not annoyed by it. They're not driven to beat it.

You understand? They're not driven to be where that person was. You need to be annoyed. And I'm telling you, I'm telling you to be angry. Anger is a fantastic force. Like I said, the world tells you not to be arrogant and not to be angry. It's two things it tells you not to do. Don't be arrogant. Don't have an ego. And don't have anger.

You're a fucking man. You're a full grown man. It's perfectly fine to be pissed off. It's perfectly fine if you look around at your life, look at the girl you're fucking, look at the house you live in, look at the car you drive and get pissed off.

You know what I want? I want a hotter bitch, I want a fucking nicer house and I want a faster car. There's nothing wrong if you take that anger and you direct it in the correct direction.

This is the reason I stopped fighting now. Because I fought and I went through hell to get everything I now have. I had nothing when I fought, I had nothing, and I wanted the life I now have. Now I wake up in one of my three mansions with one of my seven Supercars and one of my fifteen women.

WHAT DO I need to fight for? People have different motivations for different things. But my motivation was I was pissed off at the world, and now I'm not as angry as I used to be, so I don't believe I'm as good as a fighter as I used to be. I can whoop some ass. But I am not as good as I used to be, so that's why I decided to retire earlier.

But it is the second thing. The first thing, believe you're the man. Second thing, you need to get angry about your situation. Get pissed off.

Do you have a Ferrari on your drive? Get pissed off. If you don't have ten Playboy Bunny level beauties, get pissed off. You need to sit there and realise you have a few years of consciousness. You have a few short years as a young man, because age will damage you.

If you're a millionaire and you're 60 it's not nearly as good as being a millionaire at my age. I became a millionaire at 28. So you need to realise you got a few short years as a young man. You're fucking wasting them. You need to sit there and go "Fuck, shit, get angry!", because forced, directed anger is extremely powerful.

THESE ARE the first two things you need to do for a G mindset.

This is the third thing, and this is a very, very important thing because I try and explain this to people and they don't seem to understand it. So I'm gonna make this very, very blunt.

Nobody, absolutely nobody gives a fuck about you as much as you're going to have to give a fuck about yourself. Nobody cares about you as much as they need to care to fix your life. Even your parents, even your friends, even all the people who think they care about you. They care about you yeah, sure, there may be two or three people on the planet that genuinely care about you.

But nobody is going to come to your bed, drag you out of bed, fucking drag you to a job, force you to work hard, go and get you a hot bitch and go and buy you a Ferrari. Nobody is going to do that for you. You are never going to have any of the things you want, if you do not get them yourself. Nobody cares about you enough to do it for you. This is absolutely true.

PERSONALLY, I'm an atheist, and when I say I'm an atheist, people seem to be a bit confused by this. I don't know why that surprises people, but I'm absolutely and utterly an atheist. And the reason I'm atheist is because I believe that there is no grand plan, there's no God in the sky looking out for me.

I don't believe that there's anyone here to save me on this planet, or in the sky, or anywhere else. It's just me.

I have maybe, if I am lucky, 70 years, because I'm quite big, and when you're physically large, you die sooner. So 70 years of consciousness. And in these years I experience, the only person who's gonna make them fun and exciting and interesting, the only person who's gonna make me happy and live a life that I want to live, is me.

Nobody's gonna do it for me. No God has a plan for me. There's no one else who wakes up each day and goes, "You know what, I wanna make Andrew Tate's life better. I want to get him more pussy and more money".

No one thinks that about me. No one thinks that about you either. Nobody thinks that about you. The only person who gives a shit about your life truly is you. And if you don't give a shit, then you're fucked.

You're gonna start giving a shit very soon. And after you get angry, you need to realise that nobody is gonna give you the things you want. It doesn't matter if Donald Trump is the President or not. I'm a huge Trump fan, but it doesn't make a difference. No politician is going to make you rich. No one else is gonna come along and concentrate their effort on fixing your life. Nobody. You have to understand. You are out here alone.

Absolutely alone. And when you understand these three things, you start to see how a mindset comes together.

Realise nobody's gonna save you. You're fucked. It is totally down to you.

You're pissed off with your current situation and you want to change it.

And now you believe you can do absolutely anything.

This is how I thought at 18 years old. This is how I achieved so much in the short years. This is how I went from a nobody, to a world level athlete and a multi millionaire. Also people confuse the two. Kickboxing is not boxing. I made across my entire career in kickboxing maybe £700.000. I now have millions. This was not made in kickboxing. This is made in other ventures.

I have managed to be a world level athlete and extremely successful businessman at exactly the same time. Because at a very young age, when I had my prime resource of energy and power at 18, 19 years old, I understood those three tenets.

I believe I can do anything. I'm pissed off. I don't have the life that I want, and nobody else is going to give it to me. These are three things you need to understand. If any one of these elements is missing, you'll never have the right mindset. The G mindset will never formulate, if any one of these elements is missing.

ALL THREE ARE ABSOLUTELY ESSENTIAL. And the sooner you get your act together, the sooner you start to panic and worry and be concerned that you're 24, 25, you're not fucking rich yet. There's 24 and 25 year olds out there who got a contract for the fucking NBA, or have rich parents, or they won the lottery, or who knows what?

These are 24 and 25 year olds who are multi millionaires, fucking the hot models. All these Instagram girls with 3 million followers, they're getting dicked by someone and it ain't you. And that needs to piss you off. You have to get concerned, you need to get worried, you have to think "Shit. I'm running out of time!"

YOU NEED to get some urgency in your life. Put these three things together. It's absolutely essential. It's the beginning of the G mindset. When you have these three things totally done, I'll tell you what happens. I'll tell you, what happened for me.

So I became a Sayer. My brother used to say "You've become a Sayer".

And what that means is I made a pact to him that my word was unbreakable. It's strength and honour. And that if I said something, I meant it. So I'd wake up in the morning, and I'd say to Tristan that I'm doing a thousand push ups today.

Once I said it, once I spoke it, it's like a genie. It became true. If I said I was going to do a thousand push ups, I'd do them. Because if I didn't do them, I feel guilty within myself that I was the kind of person who talks shit. Because Gs don't talk shit. So the three tenets we've already learned, and you have still these in your mind. You don't want to be the kind of person who talks shit. So if I woke up and said to my brother that I'm doing a thousand push ups, or I'm running 20 miles today, I would do it.

If I didn't do it, I'd feel like a dickhead. Because when you install these mindsets, when your mindset changes, you start to be extremely accountable for yourself.

No one's coming to save you.

You have to become extremely accountable. So when you realise that your words are one of the few things you have on this planet, then if you say things, you're gonna start sticking to it.

SO THEN IT becomes very easy to train. You say you're gonna train every day this week for 2 hours a day. As soon as you said it, it's basically done. If I say something it is basically done, it's set in stone. If I say something, I'm going to do it. There's no way I'm gonna speak words into existence and then be the kind of pussy who quits because it's too hard. If I say I'm gonna do ten thousand pushups, I'm gonna do it, because I'm the kind of person who sticks to the words he says.

And this is another thing you have to understand with the G mindset. I'd be very, very specific with what you say. Because if you install your mindset correctly and you start to just say things, then you hold yourself accountable.

Say things you don't even think you want to do. Wake up and go up to your friend or whoever and say, "You know what? I'm gonna do a thousand pushups today". Say it to people. They're gonna say "No, you're not". You have a choice. You're either gonna succeed like a G, or you're gonna be a little pussy, and you're gonna quit at 310 because it's hard. What kind of man are you? That's a decision you need to make.

With the kind of man I was, I'd say shit and I'd fucking stick to it. I used to train with my brother. He said let's do 500. I'd say let's do 2000. You said it now, so you have to do it.

There is no surrender. We have to do it.

This is another factor of the G mindset. Number four, you've got to start saying shit and your word has to be iron. Unbreakable. This translates across everything in life. It's not just training, it is across everything in life, even relationships. I say to my girlfriend, "Stop fucking with me when you're out the house". Men say that all the time in arguments and then they continue to argue for two hours. They'll say that, and then they'll argue. If I say that and she continues to talk shit, I start throwing her shit out the fucking door because I said it. And if I say something, I mean it.

If I look a man in his eyes and say "Shut up or I'm gonna whoop your ass!" and he continues to talk, I have to kick his ass. I'm careful with what I say. If I tell him to shut up without the threat that's a different thing.

If I tell him i'm gonna whoop his ass and he continues to talk, I will fuck him up because I'm the kind of person if I say something, I mean what I say. I'm specific with my language and I mean every word I speak. This is another one. This is number four. You have to start meaning every word you speak.

You say to someone, "I'm gonna get rich."

You'd better fucking do it. Otherwise you're liar and you're a

The Tate Bible

ore fucking do it. You say I'm going to lift this weight, you better
fucking do it. If you're saying, "I am going to get this girl", you
better go get her. You gotta be the kind of person who says
things and means it. You promise the guy you're gonna whoop
his ass, you gotta whoop his ass. Because 99% of the people out
here talk shit. They say things they half mean or things they
don't mean.

If I say something, I fucking mean it. That is the fourth
element. You've heard the first three, this is number four. Everything you say you must mean. And once you implement that
correctly, then you get the ability to motivate yourself to no end.

You get unlimited motivation, because all you have to do is
find the energy to say it. You find the energy to say it, then you
have to do it. It's literally that easy. I wake up in the morning
and say, "Tristan, we're running 20 miles today". "Fuck's sake.
That's nearly a marathon!", "Yep, let's go". Even if it takes a
whole fucking day. I said it. If I say something, it has to happen.
This is the fourth tenet and one of the most important ones.

Because that is the power to unlimited motivation. And
that's the power to be taken seriously across all spheres of your
life. Be specific with your language.

I was in a restaurant the other day, some guy was arguing
with his girlfriend. She was talking shit and he told her "You
better be quiet, better be quiet." He kept saying this, but there
was no threat at the end of it.

I don't really like that. If you're gonna make a threat then
make a fucking threat, idiot.

But my point is, he's trying to make a threat, but he has no
real threat in the end because it's empty and the bitch is
ignoring him. All these things translate across her entire
sphere. Even on a subconscious level, they're gonna remember
that shit and your word's gonna be devalued. My word has
value. Literally I can go into, let's say the Ferrari dealership I get

my cars from, and I can say I'll pay you tomorrow and shake his hand. He'll give me the car. He knows me. I can go and get my car fixed and say I'll be back on Monday. They'll shake my hand. I don't lie and say I'll be back on Monday and then I don't have money on Monday. I'll rob a bank to make sure I have money on Monday, because I fucking said that I'd be there to pay. This is the kind of person you need to be.

So these are the first four elements of the G mindset. And these sound like simple things, but to implement them correctly in your mind, will change your entire view of the world. You will start to look at everything completely differently when you implement these four things.

If you say something, you're going to do it. Your word is iron-willed.

You understand that nobody's ever coming to save you ever.

You get pissed off that you don't have the life that you want to have.

And you couple that with I believe I can do anything.

If you truly believe all of these four things, it's going to change your entire view of this planet.

I'll wrap up quickly with probably my most famous tweet, when I had my old Cobratate account. They verified me and everything but I spoke too much truth so I was banned.

My most famous tweet, when I said depression wasn't real, and I had a list celebrities, I had the girl from Game of Thrones. I had fucking literally a list of guys. I argued with all these people and everyone told me how dangerous my mind was, and that it's dangerous to believe that you control your own mind. Because if you implement the four things I just told you, depression becomes garbage.

Depression is not a thing anymore. Feeling depressed is real. You can be depressed with your situation. I just told you, number two, get depressed. That's fine. But believing you can fix it yourself is the important key. Sitting there believing that depression is some monster from the sky that strikes your brain, and now you have no control over your life and you must take pills every day, is the absolute enemy to a G mindset.

I don't give a fuck how depressing my situation is, the only person who can change it is me.

The only person who can change how I feel about my situation, or try and affect the situation directly is me. Even if you put me in a situation, I can't change. If you put me in jail and I'm depressed because I'm in jail, I still refuse to succumb to depression. I refuse to collapse mentally and give up. I will know the only person who controls my mind is me. Nobody's coming to save me. No doctor with a pill is coming to save me. Depression isn't real.

Depression is a state of mind designed to motivate you to find a life that doesn't depress you any further.

That's all it is.

Now you have to decide, are you man enough to go and get it done, or will you sit around and cry? And depression, the reason I talk about depression a lot, is cause depression in the Western world is the best of all excuses. That is what people are using. My life is shit, because I'm depressed. No, you're depressed because your life is shit. It's the other way round and you're refusing to acknowledge that, so you want to sit there and live a shit life and pretend that some disease has struck you. And you know that's bullshit, anyone out there who's depressed. I tell you something, you're not depressed, you're a coward. And the reason you're a coward is as follows-

You desperately try to defend this crippling ailment you have. When I tell you depression isn't real, you message me pages and pages desperate to convince me I'm wrong, that depression is a real thing and that your life is terrible and this ailment has destroyed your life. You're desperate to defend your excuse.

If depression was really terrible, you wouldn't want to defend it. I'm telling you, it's not real and I know how to fix you. And if you implement a mindset like mine, you become immune to depression. If depression was so terrible, you'd listen to me and think I'll try what this guy does. If he's immune to depression, it's impossible to depress him, then I need to be like this man.

But instead, no, you don't want to do that. You want to call me names and sit and defend this ailment because you know it's garbage. It's your excuse.

It's your blankets, your shield. It's your excuse. You get to pull the same excuse out every time you look at your failure of a life. And that's why depression is absolutely not real.

I tell you something now, drop that coward bullshit. If you're reading this and you're depressed, drop and give me 200 press ups. Do 200 press ups. Look in the mirror, look in your eyes and tell yourself you're the fucking man and drop that garbage, cause you'll get absolutely nowhere in your life if you believe in that crap.

Depression absolutely isn't real. And you're gonna say this to people and they're gonna think you're fucking nuts and call you arrogant. They're gonna call you all the things they called me.

But your life is going to be a life worth living. Implement the four things I've told you, the four important tenets of a G mindset. Understand nobody's coming to save you, depression isn't real. You'll change your entire worldview once these four things are implemented correctly and then we can move on to everything else.

～

THE TRUE SECRETS TO SUCCESS

Right. So I get asked a lot about motivation and what motivates me. I think that's a stupid question. What motivates me?

Because I don't want to be a loser.

Like who wants to be a loser? I've always wanted to be rich, and I know I deserve to be rich because I see how many stupid people are rich. Look at any rapper, watch any of their interviews and see how low their IQ is. And these people are millionaires.

So if they're a millionaire, I definitely deserve to be a millionaire. I've always had motivation for the same reason, I want to be big and strong and rich, and I want to be all these things because I'm me.

I don't want be a loser.

Someone once told me that they understood that, but didn't know why I am so uncomfortable with the idea of being an average guy and having to push so hard? So I guess my typical response wasn't enough for him.

So I sat there for a little bit and I thought. What is the reason I have always been so driven my entire life? And it's obviously to do with my upbringing. But what element of my upbringing made me into such a militant individual? What made me so brilliant from a young age? I was a professional chess player, and then I became professional kickboxer, and then I became a multimillionaire business man, blah, blah, blah.

Why have I always pushed so hard? And I think one of the key elements to it is because I was always extremely proud of my last name, Tate.

And the reason for that is, in the environment I grew up around, whenever the name Tate was mentioned, people put respect on the name. When I used to go to professional chess tournaments with my father - who was one of the best chess players in the world- people would say, "Oh, shit Tate's here. Oh, man. Tate's here."

"Who's got Tate? Who's playing Tate?" Everyone was scared, and the name invoked fear. The name invoked respect automatically. Just the name Tate.

Every time something was happening to me that was difficult or challenging, I was motivated with my own last name. So if I were to say "Oh, Dad, I'm worried about this", or "Mum I'm scared about this", they said "Yeah, but you're a Tate".

Oh, yeah, I am scared, but I am a Tate.

I was state chess champion in the under 16 year olds at age five, the youngest in history. In fact, I remember being five years old and playing a whole bunch of ten year olds. There's four of them on a team against me. I remember sitting there and whooping them all.

So I was a genius. Child genius, adult genius. Whatever. But I was never told,"Oh, wow, you're so smart". For me. It was just normal. They're like, "Yeah, you're a Tate".

So they move me up three grades in school, well duh, you're a Tate. Of course, what the fuck else are they going to do? So for me, achieving things was always very, very normal. And it was always very, very easy in my mind. Of course I'll be world champion. Of course, I'll be a millionaire. Of course, I can do anything I want. And I've always believed I can do anything I want because I'm a Tate.

And I was never overtly praised. My parents were never surprised by my success. A lot of parents are very, very surprised by the success of their children. They're so happy that he's one of the best in his class. So he's one of the best of a group of 30 random, average losers? He's not top 1% in the world at anything. And you're so proud of him. And you're gonna sit there and go, wow, great job. Great job.

And that's why he's never gonna become anything. I'd be embarrassed to have a child which wasn't top 1% in the country, let alone in his shitty class. I'd be embarrassed to brag about the things you brag about. They're bare minimum acceptable standard. If I had a child and he wasn't one of the best in his class, he'd get his ass kicking. That's the bare minimum acceptable standard. And you're proud of it.

SO ONE OF the main reasons I guess I've always been so motivated, one of the reasons my life is so fantastic, is, I am one of those individuals that have it all. I was born with a genetic gift. I'm tall, caramel, sexy as fuck, rich. I can fight. I'm a genius. I got it all. And one of the reasons I've taken such marvellous advantage of my genetic gifts, and used them so beautifully and exploited them, is because I was always always cognisant that my name meant something, and I had to live up to it.

I have to succeed.

So just like in the chess halls, when the name Tate was said, now in the kickboxing world if the name Tate was said, people know, and it means something.

· · ·

YOU GUYS ARE HERE. You follow me and you watch my whole life. And if anyone else knows who I am, you say the name Tate and they know that it carries weight. And I've made it that way.

I have always blown shit out of the water without even trying. It's been easy for me, because this is how I've always been as an individual. So I guess the moral of the story is I was raised for success. And if you're sitting there and you're thinking all you want is to be more motivated, then you have two things to do.

One, stop being proud of your achievements, which are extremely minor.

And two, you need to make your name important. You need to make your name mean something.

You have to find a way to invoke a level of respect on your name.

The only way you can possibly do that is by achieving things that others cannot do.

~

TWO NAMES THAT MEAN SOMETHING TO ME

1. PRAXIS - PRACTICAL APPLICATION OF A THEORY.

2. HAYDEN. - TO BUILD UPON MY NAME.

* SOMETHING TO BE PROUD OF. I'M A HAYDEN BUT I WIN SURPASS EVERYONE.

THE SECRET TO FAST MONEY

S peed.

It's immensely powerful.

I've talked about this before. Any of you who are in the War Room, on our private networks, or students of mine. I always say lesson one is speed. Speed kills. It's nearly impossible to punch someone quickly and not hurt them.

Speed is force. Speed is fast.

If a plane is flying through the air and the engine stops. it doesn't fall. Why? Because it has speed. Speed is the only force that can defy gravity. Speed is power.

AND WHAT YOU'LL NOTICE, is that rich people live very fast lives, and poor people live very slow lives.

A poor person gets up, goes to work, sits in the traffic, comes home from work again in the traffic, watches TV. In two months he has a holiday. He's going to Spain. Has his holiday, gets up, goes back to work.

Slow.

But rich people have speed. Private jet here, dinner, back on the plane, sleeps on the plane, wakes up on a completely new continent. Dinner here, dinner there, bangs a bitch on a boat, goes there, he buys a new car. Fast, fast, fast, fast. Always doing things fast.

THE SPEED of life is dictated by the amount of money you have. In fact, I'm an extremely fast guy.

In the previous seven days of my life, I was supposed to be going on a supercar race.

The supercar race gets canceled.

So I charter a private plane to Ibiza. I stay in the most luxurious hotels in the world.

I'm chilling. This bitch hits me up on Instagram. She's saying "Come to Moscow, come to Moscow".

They won't let me in to Moscow because of Covid. I can't get a visa.

She's like, "Please come, please come". Then I see pictures of her big-ass titties and I'm like "I need to go to Moscow!"

So I hit up the War Room. "War room, I need documents!" Bang! Got a guy in Moscow who can get me in via his company. Boom! Get the visa. Bang! I fly to Moscow.

I'm pumping this hoe, then walking around Red Square like a G.

Finished there. Private plane to Warsaw, Poland. And then I thought, I haven't driven in a while. One phone call, two of my 17 supercars get sent from Romania and pull up on a truck.

I get to a five star hotel. I've got two supercars waiting for me out front.

I lay in the hotel and tag myself on Instagram, and then some Polish hoes slide into my DMs because they heard I'm in the city. So I meet up and go out with those two bitches.

Woke up this morning. Push the bitch away, went to the sauna, went to the gym, driving around the city until the police stop me. Went to Louis Vuitton. And it's Friday. What are we doing tonight? We're going to the fucking club.

Don't ask me about my life, pussy. Worry about yours.

A FAST LIFE requires a lot of money. And people often think I live a fast life because I have money to spend.

So think about something else - Not only do rich people live fast lives, but rich people have fast money. And poor people have slow money, because when you're not making very much money, you need to hold on to it for long periods of time. You need the savings in case something goes wrong. It's the first of the month and your rent is due on the 30th.

So for 29 days, you just hold onto that money, sit there and just slowly hold it. Your money is slow. Your money doesn't go anywhere with any speed. You don't have much of it. It comes in to the bank, you try not to spend it, and it just basically sits around doing nothing.

Rich people have very fast money. For rich people, the same day the money is in, it's out.

Like if you send me $100,000 right now.

I don't need to save it. I don't spend it. I don't have to pay rent. So all I do is invest it. I wanna buy something. You give me 100 grand at 9am. By 10am it's either in stocks, shares, crypto, or a car. It's gone.

Money in and money out.

People think rich people are sitting on these huge pools of money. And some of them are, perhaps the older ones. But the new generation, the young generation of rich people, they don't have huge sums of money.

They just have very fast money coming in all the time. So I

know I have a bill at the end of the month. I don't need to save for it because I get paid every single day. Every single day the money comes into my account. I know that the day before that bill comes, enough money for the bill will arrive.

IMAGINE I SAID TO YOU, you have $20,000 coming to your bank every single morning.

Every day for the rest of your life.

You would spend all that money. Every day. You would spend that money. You'd jump on private planes, you'd buy supercars. You go to the club, you spray champagne everywhere. You do whatever you want. Hotel, five star suites, bang, bang, bang. Spend the money because it doesn't matter. The next day more money comes.

That's rich. Rich is not having a big pool of money. Rich is having money coming all the time.

And when the money comes all the time, you're gonna spend it all the time. And when you spend it all the time you're gonna meet new people. And when you meet new people, they're gonna teach you.

They're gonna make connections and networks and they're gonna allow you to make even more money. So now after spending 20,000 every day, you're in Ibiza, you're on a boat. You're talking to some other millionaire. You find a way you can work together. You start working together and now you make 25,000 every day.

But the money is fast. It's coming in, it's going out quickly, Boom, boom, boom, boom boom. And the way you get richer is for more and more to turn up each day. Not to save more and more in a stagnant pool, which is what poor people do, and what poor people think rich people do.

But we don't.

My money is extremely quick. I do not hold on to money. I will never hold on to money.

What I'll do is I will spend my money to buy things that allow more money to turn up in my bank, like a rental property, or a cryptocurrency.

Or I'll spend my money on experiences and networking, which allows me to meet more rich people and then use those friendships to make even more money.

My money is a tool which I quickly destroy. I quickly blast it into an asset or an experience or a lifestyle. Something that allows me to get more money fast. Poor people get their money and hoard it like little cowards. They're afraid. So fast money and slow money are different things.

I DON'T TEACH you how to save more money in a stagnant pool, because that's not the way. If you do that, you're always going to be poor.

Think about how long it is going to take you to save a million dollars, and think how little a million dollars is. You're not even rich with a million dollars. You can't even buy most houses on my street with a million dollars.

One house. How you gonna have an appropriate portfolio? How are you going to have a supercar collection? I have $10 million of cars. You can't just save money in a stagnant pool. You need to learn how to get fast money. You have to take the money you have and buy the right things quickly.

Then when more comes in, you can use it to get even more. It's a spiral. It's a tornado that leads up to infinity. And it gets to the top where rich people like I am, and hundreds of thousands a month appears, and I'm just trying to spend it. Find me houses, find me crypto. Find me cars.

Buy a plane? Sure. Send the money away. Get rid of the money. I'm trying to spend it. My money is so quick. This is what Hustlers University is about. This is what we are going to teach you on a smaller scale. Doesn't matter if you have a 1000 dollars a month turning up. You have to start to spend that money in the right places. That will become 1200, 1400, 1600.

This is what we teach.

TATE ON FEMALE FRIENDS

A woman should never be your best friend.

Now, I know most of you guys who follow me are not little baby pussy hoes, but there are baby pussy hoes out there who consider having women as friends.

But men and women shouldn't be friends.

The reason I don't have women as friends is just because I interact with a lot females, and the interactions are as follows: There's females who I do business with etc that I know platonically, and it's just like, "Yeah, hello". Very straight and to the point. We're not friends.

For example if I go into a store as a customer and she's female, then it's just like, "Okay, yeah. Bye. Thanks."

If I'm gonna sit and talk to you and give you my brilliant personality, then I'm fucking you or I'm trying to fuck you. That's it. I don't need female friends. I'm not interested in the things females are interested in.

I DON'T SEE the point in having female friends. Any real G out there knows it's true. You got your girl or your girls. Girls you're fucking, or girls you're trying to fuck. There's no room for that other shit.

If they don't wanna fuck you, and just want to sit there and talk shit and waste your time so you can buy them dinner. No, don't do it.

I don't need female friends. If if I tell a girl we're gonna fuck and she says, "I don't want to fuck you."

OK, well, we ain't gonna talk anymore. What the fuck we gonna talk about now? We ain't gonna fuck. So what we're gonna talk about? Vampire Diaries? Get the fuck out of here.

BUT THE WORST thing about having female friends is that girls can't fight. I see those people laugh. "What do you mean, girls can't fight?"

Your boys, your friends, are your soldiers. You're out here on the mean streets. There's been 1200 stabbings in London so far this year.

Anywhere around the world, there are people out to get you, there are people out to kill you, and you're rolling with some chick. What the fuck is that? If I walk around with my girlfriend and shit goes down. It's my job to protect her, so fine. But if I'm rolling and she's just my friend. Well, it's not really my job to protect her.

If she's sucking my dick? Different. I'm not gonna get punched in the face if she won't even suck dick. No thank you. If she ain't sucking dick she doesn't get protection.

So if we're about to get jumped by these ten guys. "Lucy, what kind of combat moves do you know? How much can you bench press bitch? Because we're about to fucking fight."

Women are not combat ready. So if you're running through the world with a bunch of chicks, what you gonna do when shit goes down? Now if you sit out here going "Well, I don't actually get jumped", you probably live a boring ass life. If you live like me and you rock up in countries driving a Lambo, go to the club, spend 20 grand on champagne, walk out with some fucking ten out of ten and fuck the bitch silly, doing the shit I'm doing, then you get resentful dudes come at you.

If you're living a life worth living, and you're getting paid and laid, sooner or later, you're gonna get jumped. Now do you think it's cool to have your best friend as some chick?

You're gonna regret that shit when you eat a left hook and she's running away. Look, if I eat a left hook, I don't go down easy. My brother will be fucking coming. We'll be fighting back. In many fucking countries in the world I carry a gun.

You wanna shoot at me, we fight back. If you got a chick rolling by your side, you are not combat ready.

You are combat ineffective. And you think it's worthwhile because of the friendship, because she tells you you're really fun to talk to. You won't be talking that much at all when your jaw's broken.

Little bitch.

LIVING OFF GRID

We live in a world now of globalisation. A world where it's nearly impossible to be off grid. It's impossible to be beyond the sphere of government control if you want to live a life worth living.

You're going to need a bank account. Crypto helps a lot, but you're still in need of a bank account.

You're gonna need a passport, you're going to need a driver's license. You're going to need all of these things.

And the idea of living off grid, whether you want a very simplistic life, or a modern life, is nearly impossible. For a long time I pondered what's the best way to live off grid? What's the best way to avoid a single government having influence over me? Because one of the main reasons I don't care about politics is because I don't consider myself as having a leader.

I'm in Romania now and I don't know who the leader is, and if a leader came who I really disliked, I could move.

I LIVE in countries where I don't know who the leader is, and I don't give a shit.

So I like that. I like feeling like a citizen of the world as opposed to stuck in one place.

One of the first things I recommend you do, and this is what I did when I realised that going off grid is impossible, is actually put yourself on as many grids as you can.

I said this to some of my friends who have like, five grand in the bank. They've got five grand and want to spend it on a holiday.

I say don't. If you're gonna spend five grand on a holiday you come away with nothing. Instead spend that five grand going to another country, going into the local DVLA or the Department Of Driving or whatever it is, and find out what it takes to get a driver's license.

I say this to people and they call me crazy, but I think it's far more crazy that people don't do this. We live in a world now where if you're American, you can fly to England, or if you're in England, you can fly to America, and you can go into the office that issues documents, and you can ask what you need to do to get a driver's license.

They can say you need proof of residence, your bank account, you need X Y Z. Then you can spend a couple of weeks going through the process, getting what you need, passing the driving test and having a license in a foreign country. When I tell people to do this, they go, "Why?"

What do you mean why?

If you have one driver's license, then that country can take your license at a whim, and restrict you from moving and making money for just going 10 miles an hour over a speed limit.

People call me crazy when I say I have seven driver's licenses. I have seven licenses from seven countries. And each year I take two weeks out of my year to go to a country, get a house rental agreement, get a bank account. Anything it takes to go through the motions. Sometimes I haven't even got to do a test. Sometimes if I prove I have another license, they just give me a license.

Anything it takes to have a license, so that when I am stopped by the police for speeding, which is all the fucking time because I have a Lamborghini, Aston Martin, a Bentley, then I am prepared.

I drive how I fucking want. I'm not gonna live like a little cock. It's 50 miles an hour, but if I do 55 miles an hour they take it away from me. This is how people live under government control. Suppressed and afraid to lose their license.

If you stop me in America, I'll pull out a Polish license. What are you gonna do? Call Poland? What's the fucking officer gonna do? "You were speeding.", Yeah sorry." "I'll give you a ticket". "No problem".

You want to take my license? You have to deal with Poland about that. I don't even know how the process works if you try to take a Polish license. I don't think the American cops have a jurisdiction over a Polish license. An American cop cannot take the license of another nation. They can't do anything. Every country I'm in, I just pull out different licenses.

I GET STOPPED for speeding five times a week. No one does shit, because I have so many driver's licenses. And you guys should do the same thing.

The point of the story is, the first thing to do when you get money is you need to prevent a single government having access or control of your entire life. Same thing with passports. If I fuck up big time and England wants me in jail, I can fly with a Nigerian passport, or an American, or a Polish, or an Estonian.

I have so many fucking passports. You gonna block them all? I have four more. They can't stop me traveling. Theres always a passport I can pull out. There's always a driver's license I can pull out. If you ban one I got another one. I've got bank accounts in 19 countries.

My shit is diversified. So am I off grid? No, I'm on so many fucking grids. You can't lock the grid on me because there's too fucking many of them.

People ask me what's the first thing I should do when they get money?

I tell you the first thing you should do right now with even that little bit of money in the bank is to diversify your shit.

You'll be surprised that even a license like, for example, a Thai one is the best. You pull out a Thai driver's license and the cops are like "Is this real?" "Yeah it's real, call Bangkok!", "Ah fuck it". And they let you go.

The first thing you should do when you get money, is at least obtain two passports, at least obtain the minimum two driver's licenses, and at least as a minimum bank accounts in two different countries. Otherwise what? Otherwise, you are a little cock at the whim of one government. Let me tell you something. Governments are assholes, and governments also change.

I FIND it out absurd that you motherfuckers right now, all of you reading this right now, are driving to and from work. You need a car for your livelihood. You need a car to pay your mortgage, and you're living in a world where if you go 10 mph over the speed limit, they're gonna take that away from you. And you've done absolutely nothing to negate that.

People call me crazy for having these licenses, I think having one license is fucking crazy.

Get it done.

∾

HOW TO BE HAPPY

I get lots of emails from people who are unhappy or discontent.

"Hey, Tate, I'm really struggling", or "I'm really working at whatever, one day I want to be blah, blah."

I want you all to understand something about life. The modern world has told everyone they're supposed to be happy all of the time. And I don't think that's true, because when I get your emails I look at your Instagram and I realise you're a fat, ugly sack of shit.

Of course you're miserable. If I was you, I would be miserable. There's no happiness in your existence. Discontentment and unhappiness is supposed to motivate you. But you've been tricked by the modern world into thinking that there's a problem with you, that it's a condition, there's a disease or there's something wrong.

Completely incorrect. When you feel like shit, it's supposed to be warning you that your life is shit and something must change. And it's supposed to inspire you to push harder.

I know people who are depressed, but it inspires them to push further. They're like, "I don't want this life. Fuck this. I'm getting rich." And there's also other people who are depressed who sit there and go "I am depressed, I don't know why?" Cause you're broke, cause you're fat, cause you're a loser.

Nobody told you at any point you're supposed to be happy all of the time. You're not supposed to be happy. Happiness is on top of a mountain. And you fuckers ain't earned it.

So I am thinking of all the things that make me happy. In fact, my beautiful physique, like fucking Hercules, my Lambo, my house, these bitches, my kickboxing world titles, whatever I do, whatever I enjoy the moment. All had to be earned.

I'm trying to think what happiness has just been given to me. I can't even think of anything that can be given to you that will provide happiness over the long term. The only thing that you can be given which will provide temporary happiness is substances. And this is why people who abuse substances are doing it to try and chase one thing - happiness. Doesn't matter if it's drugs or alcohol or anything else. In fact, every addict I've ever met has been a highly emotional person.

I've met a lot of addicts, I've met a lot of alcoholics, a lot of coke addicts. I've never tried drugs in my life. I've never even tried cocaine once, but there was a period where I was selling drugs. And every single addict I met was an extremely emotional person. And when I say emotional, I mean, the kind of people who jump around nightclubs and are extremely happy but they have no stoicism.

You can always see these people in the club. "Yeah, the club!!! Britney Spears!!! Rihanna!!! Yeah yeah yeah!!!"

Morons.

I could win a hundred million dollars and I wouldn't scream like that. And these people are screaming because Rihanna is on a stage 40 metres away at a festival. No wonder the world's fucked. So extremely happy over dumb shit. They get angry or sad very quickly or for no real reason. Can't control their temper. Always talking about the past.

Ask an addict "Why are you drinking?", "Oh, man, you don't understand my life blah blah". Crying about the past. They live in the past, and they're highly emotional people, and they have no emotional control. And because they believe they're supposed to be happy all the time, they try and medicate themselves with substances. They think if they drink booze or take drugs, they will feel happy temporarily. But of course that doesn't work. It destroys their life. Everything gets worse. It's a death spiral downwards.

So my view, and I'm saying this now because I don't want to keep replying to these sad emails - but if you're not happy, you're not supposed to be happy. I'm happy because I deserve it. And if you deserve to be happy, you'd be happy too.

And that's the truth. You don't deserve happiness until you get up and you go get it. So don't email me anymore. The reason I don't want any more emails and people tell me how unhappy there are is because there's also something else we have to discuss.

Nikolai Tesla said something very interesting. And it was - If you want to understand the secrets of the universe, you must think in terms of frequency, vibration and energy.

And I, for the last couple of years have been paying very close attention to energy exchanges, and how energy is generated between people. So if I walk into a club, even if I don't do anything, I just walk in, everybody notices.

Men, women, staff. Everyone pays attention. They are now aware that I have arrived. And that happens because as the souls of humans evaporate in real time, I absorb them like Shang Tsung. I steal energy from other people. This is what I'm good at. This is what I do.

What I don't like reading are low-energy emails from low-energy people, because it's sapping.

I mean, you can't sap my powers because my G is too strong, but it's just... I don't want to read it. I don't want it in my existence. I don't want it in my realm. I'm a master of energy transfer, and I don't like that kind of energy transfer.

You have to email me things that provide me with energy, and I'll reply and provide you with energy, and we will spiral upwards while everyone else spirals downwards. This is the truth. Most people are involved in low energy activities. So let's look at the Rhianna thing we were just talking about. If you're Rhianna on stage and all these people are screaming at you, think how much energy and attention it makes.

Genuine energy is coming her way and she's absorbing it all. And you wonder why these bitches and all these celebrities look good when they're old, and why they're happy all the time now. Pseudo science, whatever.

But they're absorbing energy and attention from people, and they seem to defy age and they're happy. Whereas the people in the crowd are giving all their energy away. What are they getting back?

They're just watching a performance of a song that they could listen to on YouTube, and then they go home and they're depressed. They come down from the high and can't wait for the next one.

That's not a fair exchange of energy. You have to make sure that in everything you're doing in your life there's an exchange. I know a lot of people are reading and thinking what the fuck is Tate talking about. But you also have to understand I seem to do the impossible. I'm seeming to do the impossible in your eyes.

You have to understand. I know things you do not know. And one of the secrets in the universe is learning how to absorb the energy from other people and use it against them.

Some people are energy takers. Others are energy givers. There are producers in the world and there are consumers. And what's actually interesting is, if you talk about content, then being a producer is better than being a consumer.

But if you talk about energy, then being a consumer is better than being a producer.

So when I walk in the room, the reason everyone fucking stares, is because they can sense their powers being stolen from them. I don't even have to do anything. It's just who I am now. It's so subconscious to me. That is what I do.

When I was young, broke, and poor, and I was not nearly as important as I am today, I would go into a business meeting with someone who is far more important than me, and I would steal as much of his energy as I could in the first five seconds. And what I would do is, I would shake his hand, look him in the eye and I hold the handshake a little bit too long. He's the big rich guy, he's the boss. I'm there to pitch to him, I'm the young salesman, blah, blah, blah.

So when I did that, it was deliberately to try and steal some of his power to use against him in the exchange. You can steal people's power. Why do you think fighters look each other in the eyes before they fight? You ever fucked a bitch and look her directly in the eyes? This shit's real.

So back to the original point. If you're unhappy, you deserve it because you are not absorbing energy from other individuals. You need to find a way to steal the energy from others. There's only so much energy in the world. You do not have enough of it.

Do not use substances to try and give you happiness, because they don't give you any genuine power. The only genuine power is to evaporate souls of lesser men.

Understand me.

～

THE TRUTH ABOUT FRUGAL PEOPLE

I'm in this area of Twitter called Money Twitter, which is like rich people who make money and explain how it's done. That kind of thing. You kind of get dragged into it if you're making cash online.

I don't make all my money online. I make money offline as well.

I make money every way it can be made. But yes I do make some money online.

So I'm in this area of Twitter. There's a couple other big names in the space, and they always advocate saving. Telling people to save every penny and use your money and invest.

And I'm out here buying supercars and flexing, you know, driving, fucking with supermodels around the world, and fine champagne, all this crazy shit.

Someone said, "Hey, why do you have such a different attitude towards money than these other rich guys?" The truth is I don't have a different attitude towards money than them. We have the same attitude towards money. We all respect money.

We work hard to earn money, and we understand that money can be used to improve your life, and money can be invested to give you more money. We all understand money from the same angle.

The reason these people are so fucking boring and don't do anything fun like I do, is because we have a different attitude towards life. One particular aspect of life to make my point, is females.

People who spend money like me have a different attitude and different relationship with females than people who spend money frugally.

These people who advocate save, save, save save, are banging sixes. They have a six, they're happy with their six. They sit at home.

If you have a six and you're happy with your six, you don't need a sports car. You don't need designer clothes. You don't need to go to the club. You don't need a cool Instagram. You don't need shit if you're banging average-ass hoes. Why would you?

But if you want to bang and sleep with and converse with the most beautiful women in the world, you need to go to where the most beautiful women in the world are. And they are in expensive places.

You need to pull up in a car which is either superior to, or on par with, the other cars in the parking lot. Which means if you're gonna go to Monaco, and you want to be talking to a Russian ten out of ten, you need to roll up in an Aston or Ferrari or a Lambo.

Understand that I am too brilliant a man. Too perfect in every single metric, too big, too strong, too smart. I can fight too well, I'm caramel. I'm beautiful. It would be a shame for me to not service these females. I am a gift to females created by the one above. That's what I am.

So what am I gonna do? Stay at home and bang a six and save my money?

No!

I'm gonna roll up, flexing. Come through, bam! Champagne, bang! Yeah. Supercar outside yeah, yeah. Five star. Boom, boom, boom. First class.

Cause I am a G.

SO THESE DUDES ARE LIKE, "Oh, just save all your money. You don't need to spend money. I made this much money and I didn't spend anything".

They're advertising to the world they don't fuck no pussy. You don't fuck no pussy that way. And if you do fuck pussy, it's not the kind of pussy I touch, my friend. It ain't my kind of pussy.

My kind of pussy is on a different echelon. I'm rolling in the highest possible echelon of female beauty. I'm a millionaire kickboxing world champion. I'm what every girl's ever fucking dreamed of.

And you're sitting there saying "I made money online and saved it all!".

Yeah, because you're banging an ugly bitch. You're banging an ugly bitch. We know it. You know it, everyone knows it.

If you think I'm wrong then put some pictures of your girls on.

Oh, no, you don't show your girls do you? I show my girls. There's a reason for that. So there's nothing to do with a different attitude towards money. It's a different attitude towards females.

If you want to sleep with the most beautiful women in the world, you need a fancy car and you need nice clothes. You need to go to expensive places and need to buy 5000 dollar dinners. Because this is where the most beautiful women in the world are. And if you think that only the gold digging girls are there. Wrong.

This is where the most beautiful women in the world are.

Those beautiful women in the world are not walking around the mall in fucking Minnesota. They're not. They're on billionaires' boats in Dubai. This is just the world we live in now. Instagram has globalised the sexual marketplace.

You can be a ten out of ten from Russia or America. It doesn't make a difference. They're all in the same places every mother-fucking summer. They're all in Mykonos, in Scorpios club with $20,000 tables.

I know. I've been there. I've done it.

So when you see a rich man like me and he's flossing and he is flexing and he's spending money, you know that's the guy who likes to fuck beautiful women. When you see a rich man who's all save, save, save, save, save, then that's a guy who's happy to fuck an average woman. Very, very average because he has no ambition.

Not me. I'm a gangster. So don't email me again and say, "Oh, why do you spend so much money?"

Beautiful women are the most expensive hobby in the world. If you want to sleep with beautiful women, that's what it takes. Everything has to be fresh and expensive.

Listen, I'm living my life. I'm a G. I'm a Don, and I'm living my life for my beautiful women.

~

THE MAN WHO TELLS YOU HOW TO
GET RICH

Imagine a man who owns a casino.

So obviously you're gonna be a bit intimidated by the man who owns a casino.

What kind of friends does he have to own a casino? Now imagine a man who owns 15 casinos. And Imagine that man was a retired four time kickboxing world champion.

He got in the ring last month after training by smoking some cigars, and kicked the fuck out of some fuck.

Imagine that man had millions of dollars in supercars.

Imagine this man living in Romania, a mafia infested country.

He just rolls up. He's respected by everyone. He goes where he wants, does what he wants. Fucks who he wants.

No one fucking talks to him. No one touches him.

Big G

IMAGINE this man is gonna teach you how the world works.

Are you ignorant enough to sit there and think that this

individual doesn't know something about life that you don't know?

Imagine this man was a certified pimp with over seventy five women, making him $10 million online. Imagine you knew a man with beautiful women in the webcam game, bitcoins on the blockchain.

And imagine this man said, "Look, I know something about the world you don't know."

Are you stupid enough to not listen to that individual?

If when I was broke, I met a casino owning pimp, world champion kick-boxer, who's affiliated up to the highest possible level. I'm talking about ten passports, political friends, mafia shit.

And he said, "I'm gonna teach you about life, I'm gonna allow you to join my network. I'm gonna give you the blueprint to absolute freedom"

You know what I would do? I would fucking listen. If Mike Tyson tried to teach you how to throw a punch, you'd pay attention.

Do not DM me any more stupid fucking questions.

If you're serious about your life and you're serious about learning from me, you just DM me: "I want to learn".

That's it.

∾

HOW SLAVES THINK

S pare a thought for everyone in lock down working from home in a shitty Western country.

You know what? I have a genuine view. My view of the world is simple. The weak have always been crushed.

It doesn't matter whether it was a religion or an ideology or a skin colour. The weak have always been subjugated and crushed. This is the law of humanity.

So when I look at people who continue to put on their mask, and have not yet woken to the fact that Covid is a scam, continue to comply and sit in their police states and obey. All I see is people who deserve to be destroyed.

This is the human way. If you're an idiot and you'll allow people to treat you like a slave, you end up a slave. Anyone with a brain has run away by now. There's a few places left in the world. One of them happening to be beautiful, sunny Dubai, where you don't have to stay at home with a mask on and be afraid to hug your own wife.

With all this crazy shit, these people deserve what's coming to them. It's slavery. It's nothing less. And you know what?

Death is not the worst thing you can hope for. Death is not the worst thing that could happen to a man.

Slavery is the worst thing that can happen to a man. And you're going to allow yourself to be a slave without realising what they've taken from you. They've taken your job. They've taken your freedom. They've taken the future financial security of your children. You have nothing to lose by standing up and rebelling. What do you have to lose?

And if you still stay at home with a mask on. Then you deserve what happens. You deserve it.

ONLY WOMEN SHOULD COOK

Of course I've been busy around the world, flying about in private jets, shooting guns in Ukraine. Helping people from hopeless situations. Making millions of dollars, driving around in sports cars, living the life, you wish you had.

But you don't have it, cause you're not good enough. You know that the universe actually gives people exactly what they deserve. The universe has given you exactly what you deserve, not a penny more or a penny less. If you deserve what I have, you'd have it, but you don't cause you're not as great as me.

ANYWAY, I talked with some guy at his house the other day. And he told me, "Tate, I wanna be rich", like every dude says. "Yeah, I'd love to live your life, driving the cars", what have you.

I've actually known him for a long time. I've known him from school, and we're sitting there chilling. I was there for about 6 hours, and he's like, "Yeah, it'd be nice one day."

Then he says "Anyway, I'm hungry, you want something to eat?" I was like, "No, I'm fine bro".

So then he gets his ass up, a full grown man, and he starts to cook himself something to eat.

Now I know you amateurs think what's the problem? This guy's just making some food. But amateurs don't understand the world, because amateurs do not analyse the world as a professional, which is what I am.

I was analysing the action of this individual and I completely understood why he will remain poor for eternity.

You're sitting here telling me you're upset that you're broke, and you're gonna spend time (and everybody knows the age old quote "Time is money", you're gonna spend time preparing food?

Now, actually, think about this for a second. If you're broke, if you're not a millionaire, the last thing you should be doing with your time is cooking. I can't think of a lower return on investment activity than walking to the fridge, getting out some ingredients and "Ooh, an onion, oh look at the onion, I'm gonna start cooking onion and some lettuce. And now I get my knife, cut my onion."

You're broke! You're fucking poor! You can get a rotisserie chicken for five bucks. Boom, chicken. Bang. Eat. Bang. Back to work.

You could fucking do a million things. You can go for a run, you can get in shape in the time you waste cooking. If you dedicate yourself to kick boxing, you could have got paid for kickboxing. Or piano. You could fucking be a traveling piano man with the time you wasted cutting fucking onions.

If you're broke, there is zero reason why you should ever prepare a meal. If you're a multimillionaire and you're a boring one, not a fun one like me driving fast cars, and you have all the time because you are rich and you want to cook? Sure. Waste your time.

But if you're not a multi millionaire, your time is extremely important as a man. It needs to be dedicated towards world conquest. There's no need to prepare food. Either order something which can be done very cheaply and very helpfully like chicken with a bag of salad for like five bucks, or instruct a female to provide sustenance. Eat and get back to world conquest. You have better things to do.

So I'm sitting there and my friend cooked his meal, and I told him "You're a jackass, you're gonna be poor forever". "What do you mean?" "Because you're cooking". "But everyone cooks. Everyone's broke". Doesn't that prove me right? That proves me totally right. I can't think of a more stupid thing to do.

So you gotta ask yourself this question. Are you broke? Yes. Do you cook? Probably. Do you not see the problem here? That is a complete waste of your human time. The cooking, the preparation, the cleaning up afterwards. You're gonna do this three times a day. What the fuck is wrong with you?

So this became my new world view, and I'm going around telling everybody, "You're broke, you cook, you're a jackass". "You ain't got a Lambo? I bet you cook food, don't you?" Boom, boom, boom.

Some fucking dork thinks he's a tough guy, that a real man cooks a real steak. But do you know what a real man actually does? A real man gets in the cage, a real man becomes a four-time kickboxing world champion.

A real man has millions. A real man has supercars. A real man has a property portfolio. A real man has the police chief of the city he lives in on fucking speed dial. That's what a real man does.

A real man doesn't sit in his fucking broke-ass house with his ugly-ass wife, cooking steak.

That's bullshit. You think you're a real man because you managed to cook a steak? That is a cop out.

It's the ultimate symbol of failure if you're gonna say that your credentials for masculinity are putting meat on a fucking stove. Do you know how I cook a steak, as a real man? I instruct one of my seven girlfriends "Meat, now!" Boom, it turns up perfect with tabasco on the side, and a nice glass of ice water.

I do shit. That's how a real man cooks his steak. If you think cooking is important or manly, or it's a good, tough way to waste your time, a good pastime, or even sitting there going "Well, I need to eat, so I'll just cook" - You do not understand the true link between genuine focus on an objective and success.

Because I promise you, when I was broke, I didn't have time to cook.

I was too busy learning how to get fucking rich.

∾

WHAT YOU SHOULD NEVER DO ON INSTAGRAM

Here's something you should never, ever do...

Do not watch other people's Instagram stories. Don't do it. I have never in my life watched someone else's Instagram story and improved my life or my mood.

Cause it's one of probably two things. Inane boring bullshit that doesn't interest you, or something amazing going on to make you feel that little bit of jealousy and envy. No one's gonna update their story with bad news.

It's gonna be somebody who just bought a brand new Lambo, or be somebody just about to dive off a fucking water-fall. Or it's gonna be someone singing along to a song. Some bullshit. So it's either bullshit or something that's gonna piss you off.

WATCHING people's Instagram stories is completely and utterly a waste of time. I do not see anything positive that can come from it. You should only be digesting information that's going to improve you as a person or improve your mood. And me personally, I just do not see any mood improvement ever from Instagram stories.

And of course there's a caveat for this, because if you follow me on Instagram, you should watch my stories because I'm the fucking man. But besides me, there's absolutely no need to watch that shit.

WE'RE in Moldova with these three girls, me and Tristan. One of them is bored and she's on Instagram just scrolling through stories for an hour. She's digesting pure garbage. Garbage through the pixels into her retinas, being processed by her brain. How many of you do that?

I'm guilty of it. I'll admit it myself I'm a phone addict. I'll admit that myself. I'm constantly on my phone.

If I'm awake on my phone, my phone's on silent, but I will still reply instantly because I just live on my phone. I'm bad for it, I know I am, and sometimes I catch myself just scrolling through Facebook. Just scrolling through absolute shit.

You have to consciously prevent yourself from doing that. Do not scroll up and down Facebook.

It's garbage. Do not look through Instagram stories, it's garbage. Delete Snapchat. That shit's pure garbage. You need to get all that shit out of your fucking life. It cannot improve your life in any way. I use Instagram, and I update my story. I am the main character in my life.

I don't give a fuck about anyone else's life but mine. On my Instagram I put it out there what I am doing. If you want to follow me, this is all up to you. But my number one tip to you if you're looking to improve your life is, besides me obviously, stop looking at everyone else's shit. Why give a fuck if it ain't getting you paid,? Why do you give a fuck what other people are doing?

. . .

IF YOU WANT an interesting Instagram story to watch, you should be able to watch your own. And if it's not interesting enough, do something about it. I see so many dudes out there living their lives vicariously. Fucking processing information on bullshit that other people have done.

Probably about three years ago I was out on a date with some girl.

She was boring. They're all boring.

But I was listening because I'm perspicacious and I'm also hyper-intelligent. I can have a conversation with a bimbo while also hearing other conversations in the room.

So I was talking to this bitch while also listening to the table next to me, and on the table next to me, there was man and a woman who were on their first date, and they were getting to know each other.

But the way they were getting to know each other wasn't about who they were as people. It was all vicarious bullshit of how they enjoy other people's achievements, or how they live through other people.

"So what's your favourite band? Oh, I like these people. Well I like these people", etc

Have you ever been to see this person in concert? Have you ever been to this festival?

None of it was "I have done this". It was just "I like the achievements of this person. Do you like the achievements of this person? I like when when this other person does something. Do you like when that other person does something?"

It's like their whole personality was outsourced to the achievements of other people. They wouldn't even be the main character if a movie was made about their lives.

The main character would be some band or some football team or some garbage, it's bullshit. Why would you give that much dedication and attention to someone that doesn't even know you exist? It's insane. And Instagram is exactly the same.

You can take this train of thought and extrapolate it out. When I say I've never been to a concert people look at me and ask why? Because that person up on stage doesn't give a fuck if I go or not.

Why am I going to spend my money making someone else rich? If I got cancer and I sent them a message on Instagram that I have cancer and I need $1 for me to live, they'd ignore my message. They'd leave it on read and I'd die because they wouldn't give me a dollar. But I'll give them $100 of mine for a concert?

When people hear this they go, "Oh yeah, but when you're kickboxing you need fans to come see you". Yeah, you're right. I do need fans to come see me. I'm lucky people do think that way or I wouldn't have made any money. But me personally, as an individual, if I care about music, I'll write my own music.

I enjoy listening to music, everyone likes music. I'll put music on the car, I'll put it on for free. I put on the radio. I'll put on YouTube. But I'm not gonna go out of my way to make someone else rich. I won't stand there in a crowd, jump up and down like that person is Jesus?

They don't know I even exist.

And Instagram is exactly the same shit. Most of these people whose stories you're watching don't give a fuck about you. If you got run over by a car tomorrow, would they even mention it? Would it slow them down? Or would they be too busy fucking at night, and all the other shit they do without a care in the world.

You want to sit there and fucking digest their life? Oh, they wouldn't give a fuck if I got run over by cement mixer. But here I am. Let me just watch what they did today.

Cut that garbage out.

∾

THE FUTURE OF THE WEST

I'm not scared of Covid.

Let me have it. It's fine.

I'm not gonna get the jab. And the reason for that is, I don't believe that anybody else has my best interests at heart. I don't believe that my school really cared about me. I don't believe that governments really care about me. I don't believe that AstraZeneca with their vaccine really care about me. I believe the only person who genuinely cares about me and my life is me.

I believe the only person who wakes up each day and goes, "You know what? Let's put some money in Andrew Tate's bank", is Andrew Tate. I believe that when stuff really hits the fan, you're gonna fuck off and look around, and you might have one or two close people. But in general, you are by yourself.

I DON'T TRUST anybody else. So when a government comes along and says you need to live this way, I realise that's not for the benefit of me. That's for the benefit of the government.

When AstraZeneca says, "You need this injection", they

don't care if I have Covid. They want billions and billions of dollars like every other huge company in the world.

This is the fastest vaccine that's been produced in history.

It takes years to produce a vaccine. The fastest vaccine before this one took eight years. This one's pulled off in less than a year. You're just going to tell me they haven't cut a single corner? And if someone does get sick from the vaccine, the media won't report it, because the media works with the pharmaceutical companies.

So nobody knows what's happening with this injection. And I know I don't need it, so I refuse to take it.

I know that nobody else has my best interest at heart but me. So for that reason, I'm a rebel, right? A government cares about its people the same way that a farmer cares about its cows. It wants the milk, it wants them alive. It wants them healthy enough to slaughter and sell. But it doesn't really care if they're happy or not. No one cares that the majority of men out there are working slave jobs and are depressed, and their wife won't even give them a hand job. No one cares about them.

Nobody cares about people, right? So I only care about myself. And that's made me a rebel because I only trust me. I trust me. And that's why I can't be programmed.

If I get Covid and have a really bad experience and then I say "Okay, you know what, Covid is serious I believe I need an injection", then I will go get one. But the fact that throughout this entire year, nothing bad has happened to me, despite me breaking every single rule, then I don't see why I'd inject something into myself. I don't care what it is. I don't see the point of it. So, yeah, maybe I am a rebel. I don't have any faith.

BEFORE I GOT RICH, when I was kind of like, average income, I thought the rich and the elite of the world were these hyperintelligent people.

But now I've sat around the Bugatti table. I've sat there with the other ten people who bought $5 million cars. And let me tell you something-

These are not smart people. They're not amazing human specimens. They're fat, they're lazy. They were late. They're drunk and sloppy. You would think that people at the top would be better than the average person. They're not. The people who work for AstraZeneca are not amazing people. They're just normal humans with marriage problems, and they're semi-depressed, sitting in traffic like everybody else.

And the idea that these people will never make a mistake, or that these people are beyond corruption, that they won't sit there and go "Oh, well, the vaccine won't hurt most people, a few people will die, but we'll make billions". Do you really believe that these people are good in their hearts? They don't care. Nobody cares.

That's the way the world works. And the people at the very top have never cared. They locked us all in our houses and destroyed everyone's income. They didn't care. They don't care about us.

So I'm a rebel because I don't trust these people. I don't trust them. That's all it is. It's just a matter of I only trust myself and people that I know and have a track record with. Those who have been there for me when I need them to be. So for that reason, I don't trust very much.

I THINK Eastern Europe is the place to be. I think Eastern Europe is the future of Europe. I think that as Western European countries decline, Eastern European countries are on the way up because they have strong borders and they have strong nationalistic tendencies. Countries like Poland, Slovakia, Romania. They're very nationalistic. They fly the flag.

You must respect their country. You can't go there and talk

bad about their country. And I think this is a good place to be. I like all of them, but I prefer Romania the most.

Romania is the least civilised of them all. Poland is very very civilised, very clean. Romania is, like, 20 years behind. It's not civilised, and it's also very chaotic and very corrupt, but that suits me because I have money.

I like living in a corrupt place when I have money. So if I want to drive at 300 miles an hour, as long as I have money in my pocket, it's not a problem. So I like it here for that reason.

I do not think Romania will leave the EU because Romania is taking billions and billions and billions of taxpayer money from Germany to build highways which never get built and goes missing in corruption scandals. So it's all over the news here. Every single year, billions go missing in corruption scandals. So the Romanian government are just robbing the European Union. So for that reason, I don't think they're going to leave. The EU influence on Romania is real and it is starting to get a lot stricter.

For example there used to be basically no speed limit. Now they have speed traps. So things are starting to change here. The EU is starting to get in. But I don't think they're going to leave. I think they're just going to milk it for as long as they can.

But I am super impressed by Belarus. I couldn't believe it. Clean, beautiful, nice streets, organised traffic, perfect. Nice cars, Mercedes, BMWs. It was like it was beautiful, super safe.

Belarus super impressed me. So there's other countries to go to where you haven't got to worry about. I can wear a quarter of a million dollar watch in Romania, Dubai, and Belarus. I would never wear one in London. Never in a million years.

So there's certain places in the world which are still very, very safe, and a good place to live. Romania is one of them.

But if that changes, I'll just keep heading East. If I end up in Moscow, I end up in Moscow.

I refuse to live in a society where the police are going to give me trouble for what I say. I refuse to live in that society. I don't think that's a fair place for me to pay my taxes. I refuse to do that. So whatever it is, I'm not going back to England.

I'll leave it at that.

THE PANDEMIC HAS REMOVED the last faith I had in humanity. You look at World War Two, and everyone asked how the German people allowed the Nazis to do that? And the answer is, well, the German people just did as they were told. And then you look at the Covid pandemic and you see people just doing as they are told. Ignoring their eyes, ignoring their ears.

Like at the beginning of this, we saw all the videos of people in China falling over, dying. Nobody has actually seen that. You haven't seen anyone dying in the street. The hospitals are not full. You can go to the hospital right now. The hospitals are empty. There's no full hospital beds. Everyone's fine.

But because the news says pandemic, people still believe they're living in a pandemic. They don't trust their own eyes. They don't trust their own ears because the government has told them, just like the Nazis told the Germans "These people are bad, those people are bad. Do this. Do that".

So I very much understand how the Nazis got away with what they did, because the pandemic has proven that people have not learned a single thing. Nobody will wake up and look around and do what I did. I travel the world, look for myself, see with my own eyes, and realise I don't see any sick people.

But they cry "Oh, the Covid deaths. the Covid deaths". Yeah, but the deaths of the flu have gone down to zero. You just label all the flu deaths as Covid deaths. Everyone knows that. Everybody knows that because the flu deaths have gone from X amount a year to zero. Everyone knows what's happened.

But people are still sitting here going, "Ohhh the pandemic". There is no pandemic. So I am really amazed at how far this lie has continued.

I'm also amazed at how quickly everybody complied. I was saying this at the very start, and people were calling me completely crazy.

They deleted me from Facebook. They would never talk to me again. I was a dangerous individual for telling them that nobody should lock you in your house. I'm telling you, no one should lock you in your house and you're mad at me? The majority of people are conditioned for slavery, and I mean that without disrespect.

Most people are so dependent on the system, they will fight to protect it. They're conditioned to just obey and comply, and to work a job which doesn't reward them, just to make a little bit of money. And that money is worth less every single year, and the price of important things like houses and land goes up every single year, but their wages never go up. So they're going to sit there and stay broke and stay a slave forever. This is how their mind is programmed.

This is what they're conditioned for. Most people are not really willing to wake up and look around them and understand what's happening, because the world is splitting right now. There's going be elites. There's gonna be people like me who can jump on a private jet with his fourth passport and go wherever he wants. And there's people who are still locked in their house because of quarantine.

There's two types of people. There's people living two different lives right now. When I was flying on private planes, no one told me to wear a mask. Nobody asks for quarantine paperwork. Nobody cares. Just because I was rich. This is what people don't understand. The world is splitting right now. Do you think all the people who make the Covid rules actually listen to the Covid rules? No, it is in the paper every single day. We catch some Minister breaking the Covid rules.

They're locking you in your house but they're disobeying. And people are not waking up yet to the fact that slavery is coming for those who are stupid enough to just blindly comply with the lies that are being told to them on television.

So Covid has just proved to me that most of the world doesn't stand a chance. Most people are not really capable of thinking for themselves. And as for the future of the West, this is the same thing. The West is in decline because of all the things we can't discuss. We can't talk about how political correctness has destroyed our ability for men to stand up and say what they believe in.

You can't even be nationalist anymore. You can't even be an English person who loves England and wants England to be English. And for people to talk your language. You can't do anything.

And this is the future of the West, because if you do those things, you are labelled a bad person. The news tells you you're a bad person. The TV, the brainwashing, the comply, comply, comply, comply. The future of the West is slaves who comply and elites who ignore all the rules.

Crime is spiralling out of control and there's land and property that no one can afford, and ever shrinking wages as most jobs go to robots. That's the future of the West and thats why I left.

~

HOW TO AVOID MAIL

You know what's cool about being rich?

Nobody can send me mail.

When I was broke I hated mail.

When I was the most poor, when I had debts I hadn't paid, court fines, when I was really in trouble and the rent wasn't paid....BROKE!

I HATED the mail. Every time the mail man passed i'd pray I wouldn't get any letters.

But i'd get a stack telling me "You should've been here", " You should've paid this and now it's more", "You owe us this money now." Fuck!

I HAVE NEVER ONCE OPENED a piece of mail and it was like "Hi Andrew, here's some money". Never!

It was always "Hi Andrew, GIVE me money". All the time.

So when I was broke I thought "When I get rich, I'm gonna make sure that nobody can send me mail".

I don't want it. I've never had anything good come in the mail. It's always a court date - "You killed this guy, you drove at

200mph down the fucking highway", "You owe us this much because of whatever".

It's bullshit.

I'm sure right now even with my net worth of millions, if I had a place for people to send me mail, they'd be sending me pieces of paper telling me I owe them shit. Or I have to be somewhere. Or I broke the speed limit in Austria.

So yes I got stopped for speeding in Austria last month. But has anyone talked to me about it since?

No!

Why?

Because you can't send me mail. If I had a mailbox there'd be some Austrian letter with a load of bullshit.

Maybe i'm a wanted fugitive in Austria. Who the fuck knows, who the fuck cares? Maybe I'm supposed to be in court today. But I'm not. You know why? Because I have no mailbox.

I SAY AGAIN, when i was broke I thought "When I get rich i'm not gonna let anyone send me mail."

And by coincidence I now live in Romania which has a terrible postal system anyway, and I have a bunch of properties that no one knows the address of and where to send stuff to. So now nobody can really send me mail.

Even the ways my cars are registered and set up, you'd just end up looking up the numberplate and finding some limited company and sending a letter to......no one.

No one's going to open it.

Sorry Austrians. Sorry. No one's opening your crap.

Mail is trash.

And only broke people receive it. The rich man doesn't have to receive mail.

If you really want to talk to me and it's that important then you'll find a way.

But i'll tell you what, getting a piece of paper and writing "Andrew Tate give us money" on it, and then a few days later me receiving it and actually paying them... that would make me a loser.

Don't you see that's how the world works? You're a loser.

Someone out there goes "Hmmm.. Joe Shmow. Fuck Joe Shmow enjoying his nice car on a nice road. Fuck him. No fun allowed so pay me this". Look on the computer at the peon database. There he is Joe Shmow, Dork Road. Send it!!

Two days later Joe Shmow gets the phone call, finds his credit card and PAYS them.

YOU'RE A LOSER!

With me they're like "Andrew Tate has broken ALL the rules. Let's send letters to all 25 of these addresses". No reply. They send them again. No reply. "Right let's put up the price and threaten him. We'll send bailiffs and recover assets...SEND!"

Do you understand?!

That little fucking bitch behind that desk can send letters for the next two hundred fucking years.

You ain't gonna take my stuff, I'm not gonna open your fucking letters, so fuck you and fuck the mail.

TATE ON THE TIMESCALE OF SUCCESS

I saw something on Twitter the other day and it was about Timescales Of Success.

And it was saying that Morgan Freeman didn't get his first acting job till he was 50, or there's a guy who's a millionaire at 20 but dies at 30, and there's a guy who becomes a millionaire at 40 but dies at 80, and all this bullshit.

It basically comes out and says you work to your own timescale, you're not under any pressure. And I sat there and I thought "Well, that's bullshit". That's some fucking make yourself feel better with your shit life garbage.

Because we all have one timescale, and that timescale is the human timescale. None of you are going to leave it that long. We're all going to be dead in about 70 to 80 years. So you do have a timescale, and you do have a time limit.

On top of that, life when you're young is a completely different experience to life when you're old. Having $5 million when you're young is much better than having billions when you're 70. What the fuck are you going to do with money when you're old? Your dick doesn't work. You're tired. You don't want to go places. You're decrepit. You're slow. There's nothing left to do at that age unless you're a G like Trump. You can become President, piss everyone off, like a fucking hero.

But in general, when you're older, your life quality seriously decreases massively. So it's not even 80 years of time you have to be successful. You have half of that to be successful. You're not smart enough to try and start something when you're 15 or whatever, unless you're like that little fuck on YouTube I've seen making 22 mill a year.

So you have about 10 to 15, maybe 20 years to find a way to get rich and enjoy being rich. And you've got to put it all together and do it quick. It ain't fucking easy.

So when I see these success timescales... That's complete bullshit and it's absolutely not true. I don't think any of you people should be living in a fucking dream. I don't think living in a dream is going to help you in any way. I think you need to be sitting here panicking at the fact that you don't have enough money. You need to be concerned and worried and sad, and you need to do something about it today.

Because that's how I started my first business that made me a million dollars: I sat in my room pissed-off, and I came up with an idea. Because there's none of this "I'll being successful when I'm older" bullshit. One day you are going to die. Or if you're very lucky, you're going to be successful by the time you're too old to enjoy.

When I drive my Lamborghini, the reason everyone stares is because there's a young man in the Lamborghini. If I had grey hair, no one would give a fuck. Oh, it took 65 years and you can afford a car... As opposed to who the fuck is young stallion? Who's this G pushing this car? What the fuck is he doing?

And that's how you need to live your life.

～

TATE ON THE METOO MOVEMENT

MeToo, the sexual assault bullshit, has fucked up the western world.

The western world is finished because of this garbage. We need to put a stop to it instantly, and what we need to do is as follows. Pay attention, get a pen and paper. Tate's talking.

You need to put a time limit on sexual assault allegations. You do this for two reasons:

One, it prevents fucking psychos coming up with accusations from 33 years ago which can never possibly be proved or disproved. You can never prove or disprove something from 30 years ago. There's no physical evidence. It's your word against theirs. It's garbage. Let's end that shit.

Two, it'll inspire people to come forward straight away if there is a genuine incident and a genuine allegation. I suppose these girls go "Well, I was scared to say anything. But now that I'm 68 and I might get some money from Trump, I've now found the courage".

Fuck that shit. There needs to be a time limit. And I'd put adverts all over the TV saying if something bad happens to you come to the police instantly so we can check CCTV footage from the night before, so we can get physical evidence of a wrongdoing. Not 30 years later.

And I've said this to people before and they go "Yeah, girls sometimes need time to build up bravery". Well, they haven't got time for that shit. We're going to make it clear. If something bad happens, you go to the police fucking straight away so we can catch the bad guy.

I completely do not believe women should be victims to rape or any kind of sexual assault. But I also don't believe men should be held hostage to the fact that any woman you've ever interacted with in your life ever, at any point in the future, even 40 years later, can come forward and accuse you of something and fuck your life up.

Because the problem is it's supposed to be innocent until proven guilty. But with this sexual assault bullshit, you're guilty until proven innocent. If a girl comes forward and claims "He raped me back in 1988", you're a rapist. They have no proof, it hasn't gone to court, you haven't been convicted. But you're a rapist in everyone's eyes until you somehow prove she's lying.

How the fuck am I going to prove a bitch is lying about something that happened in 1988? But for the same reason she can't prove it happened, I can't prove it didn't happen, and then you're just stuck with a fucking smear campaign, a bunch of garbage when you haven't even done anything wrong.

I've said this to girls before and they sit there and go, "You know what, if you go through life and you're just really respectful to women, you have nothing to worry about".

That's not true. And I'll tell you why. Because what we've done is we've weaponised sexual assault allegations. They've been weaponised. We've given every female in the western world a weapon. And that weapon does not have to be used fairly. That weapon can be used completely unfairly. You can go through life and treat women with respect, and be a really good guy.

But the MeToo era is saying you can never piss off a female ever, because if you do, they have a weaponised response.

It's not that you have to go through life and make sure you never assault a woman. The reality is you have to make sure you go through life and never make a woman angry, ever, because if you make her angry she might just call the police.

Don't ever dump a girlfriend. You're not allowed to dump her. Don't ever ignore her texts. Don't ever owe her 200 quid for a bit too long because she'll call up the police and fuck your whole life up. You'll lose your job. You'll fucking be on bail and be looking at all this stress and headache with zero evidence.

So what you're saying is we can never ever, ever upset a woman ever? What if I have a girlfriend and I never ever sexually assaulted her? I never put my hands on her, but she doesn't suck dick very good and I say "Bye I don't want to be with you anymore?" Then what? Have I committed a crime? No. I just don't want to be with her. For the same reason if a woman didn't want to be with a man, she'd be completely in her rights to say I don't want to be with this guy anymore. If I had to try and force her, I'd be a psycho.

Well, imagine that this has happened, that you've said to girl, I don't want to be with you anymore, and the girl's constantly chasing you, texting you, and then she thinks "You know what, fuck this guy", and decides to go to the police with an accusation. Then what? You've done nothing wrong. You've done absolutely nothing wrong. But she has a weapon she can use against you at any point. It's insane.

I'm at the point now that when I talk to girls in the West, I have to fucking archive my text messages. I got shit fucking archived... If you've got money, this shit happens. Make 10 mil, this shit's going to happen to you.

If a girl wants to go to the police about me now, I'll be like alright, wait, wait, wait, I'll open up that folder, here look, prove she's a bimbo. Why do I have to live that way? Isn't that insane?

This is probably 40% of the reason I moved to Romania, because in Eastern Europe, none of this garbage flies. If you're going to go the police and say he raped me back in 1988, they'll say you should have done something about it back then.

If you tell the police you were raped yesterday, they'll ask if you have got physical evidence or is there CCTV proof where it happened? Okay, let's go interview him right now. And if the truth is simply that we went to the club, we got drunk, she agreed to go back to my house, we started having sex and she didn't say anything was wrong, and she was all fine and texted me afterwards, but I didn't text back, and now she's saying I raped her. The police would be like okay, she's an idiot. Bye. But no, not in the West.

In the West, you can tell that exact story, but you're still fucked. You're fucked in the West.

If you have sex with a girl and decide to not have sex with her again, and she's upset about it, she can just decide to go "It's rape now". A girl can get drunk with you in the club, have sex with you consensually, have sex with you again two days later, you can see each other on and off for two weeks and you can fuck all the time. Then you can decide you don't want to see her anymore, she can be obsessed with you and she can think "You know what, well, the first time we had sex I was drunk, so he raped me". And then she goes to the police and accuses you of rape and your life's over.

On what planet does that make any fucking sense? So if you live in the western world, you have to understand that any female you have ever interacted with, ever, at any point in the past or future, if you piss her off, she has the ability to destroy your life. Are you happy to live under those conditions?

People ask why I live in Romania and I explain my reasons. One of them is the MeToo era. They go "Oh, well, you're a rapist". I say "No, I'm not a rapist. But I like the idea of being able to do what I want. I like being free. I like being able to say to a girl, I don't want to see you anymore. Done.

The point is, I don't like knowing that any woman I've ever spoken to can destroy my life. And if you're a man living in England, or Germany, or America, or any of the Western world right now; then you've decided to live in a country where any woman, any ex, any fucking bitch who works at Gregg's who you bought a pastie from, at some point in the future, can destroy your life.

And you're sitting there thinking "Oh, but they won't do it". Some won't, but some will. It's not about whether they will, it's about whether they can, because sooner or later if people can, they will.

And I'm telling you now, this is going to happen to at least a percentage of you reading this, it's going to happen to you.

And you're going to be sitting thinking "That Tate guy he ain't fucking dumb. He told me, it's right".

Brett Kavanaugh, nominated for Supreme Court Justice, had some bitch come out and say he fucking tried to touch her leg in 1978. Nearly didn't get the job. It's crazy.

This MeToo era has not protected women, it's just destroyed the safety of men. It's no longer safe to be a heterosexual male who enjoys sex in the Western world. It is no longer safe.

WHY THEY HATE TATE

Paul Joseph Watson: I'm here with Andrew Tate, four-time kickboxing world champion. He's the son of the chess grandmaster Emory Tate. He's also a commentator, businessman, multi-millionaire, and all-around G. Andrew, good to have you here.

Andrew: Absolutely, man, it's a pleasure to be with such a fine gentleman such as yourself.

Paul: Now this is going to be obviously a relaxed chat. It's not going to be a structured interview. So people can watch it in the background, they can go about their daily activities and enjoy it. But I'm going to call it "Why Do They Hate Andrew Tate?" I did a video the other day "Why Do They Hate PewDiePie?" I'm going to do a series, I think, of why people who get in the public eye and are so castigated, so dragged down, what threat they pose to the media, to the establishment. So it's a broad question and feel free to take it off in any direction.

Because you know, we're constantly lectured in the culture about not being divisive, never be divisive. The most interesting people on the internet are often or almost always the most divisive. And those are the people I want to listen to.

Andrew: Well, how could you even be interesting if your opinions are run-of-the-mill 50-50 sitting on the wall? So many people are afraid of losing their career or their sponsorship or whatever garbage. They don't even have an opinion on anything.

Paul: Well there's a whole breed of YouTubers whose job it is to sit on the fence and we all know who they are. And as he said, it's boring, nobody wants to watch it. But you're in the bracket of willing to stick your neck out the furthest on many issues, and you've done that on many different subjects in the past. You've got a web series called the "Hateful Tate". Why do people hate you?

Andrew: Okay. Well, this is buckle up, Mr. Watson time, I hope you have an hour or so?

Paul: Oh, yeah. Before you start, by the way, anyone who's going to tweet me or send messages like oh, didn't you see this tweet from him last year? I don't give a shit, okay. I don't give a shit. You don't have to agree with every opinion someone has to talk to them. Okay. So get over yourself and move on. Go ahead.

Andrew: Absolutely. So yeah, everyone hates me. We agree on that. That's a good basis to start with. But I think it's a combination of reasons. I think that one, because I embody the less liberal idea of toxic masculinity. Now, I am their arch-nemesis. I'm a six foot three kickboxing world champion millionaire who's openly sexist, who has lots of women, who drives around in his Lambo, doesn't care about social norms, and refuses to listen to anybody.

So in their mind, I am their opposite. If they're Spider-Man, I'm definitely Venom. You know, I'm everything they hate. I fight. I've got chicks. I got money. I'm riding around in my car. So this is one of the reasons.

And another reason is because I'm fortunate enough to be super anti-fragile. What normally happens is you upset somebody and then they try and upset you back. But no one can upset me. No one can get me fired from my job. No one can report me to anyone. I'm out here in Romania at the moment which is completely non-pc anyway. No one can get me fired, no one can make me apologise. I've never said sorry for anything I've ever said, ever, and they can't make me do it. And they can't make me care about them being mad at me. And that's what it really is.

If you're mad at someone, the only person who has a negative emotion is you. If you're mad at someone, you're the only person harbouring the emotion. I don't harbour the emotion if you're mad at me. I don't care. And they try and make me care and they can't, and then they just sit there poisoned and upset. "I hate this dude and he's just ignoring me", and they have small genitalia and it all just adds up and they get upset. That's how it goes. And I'm still the man. Nothing changes.

Paul: They can't get under your skin. You're the Teflon-coated Tate, and that obviously relates to the depression issue which we're going to get into in a bit. But I want to start with masculinity.

The MeToo movement, you know, there was a poll which I cite often. 25% of millennial men in the United States now think that asking to buy a woman a drink is a form of sexual harassment. 25%, one in four of us millennial men think this way. Testosterone levels are plummeting. Soy consumption is increasing. Incels are now turning to violence. People criticise us for being misogynist, but you know I've made videos criticising incels and the crisis of masculinity, which isn't all the fault of feminism or the Left. It's about taking personal responsibility.

What's your core message to young men? And you've got several courses on cobratate.com that address this. What's your core message to young men who need to reassert their masculinity but who live in a world where they're constantly told that it's toxic to do so?

Andrew: Well, absolutely, and this is what's most crazy about it. While you were talking, you raised about 10 points I want to expand on. But firstly, what's most crazy about it is this: They tell young men to act a certain way, and they say you must act more feminine, you must not act masculine, don't be this way, don't be that way. And all that does is makes them unattractive to females. Like, let's cut the garbage.

There's going to be some feminist out there who's overweight and ugly, and who's going to sit there and pretend she wants a feminine man.

But the reality is, all women know they want a masculine man. So they're saying oh, don't be this way, don't be that way. And all they're doing is effectively saying to guys you're never going to have a girlfriend, and if you do, she's going to cheat on you with Andrew Tate.

That's all they're saying. They're literally setting these people up for failure in relationships. That's the first thing.

Secondly, you're setting them up for failure in life. I mean of course, there's always some liberal garbage SJW left wing Google-type company you can work for. But in general, if you're going to go out and get a normal general job and be amongst men, you're going to need a semi-masculine attitude and mannerisms and worldview.

You know, men banter, we make fun of each other a little bit, it's fine. What's crazy about it is this: The feminists believe, and the Left believe, that they're trying to emasculate men to make men more like women. And in their mind, they're thinking that women are less threatening because women commit less violent crimes, so if they make men like women, we're going to have less violent crime. But they're ignoring two important facts.

One, men are biologically programmed for violence. And that's because from an evolutionary standpoint, we needed violence to survive. For a long portion of human history, you needed violence to protect your wife, and protect your clan and go and kill an animal. In fact, Paul, I think you did a video on this. There's many parts of the world still today where if you go there and you're incapable of violence, you're going to be in trouble. That's the first thing. So that's why men are more dangerous than women.

And then they think oh, well, if we break men down and make them more feminine, they'll just sit and watch rom-coms and they'll cry all day.

No, what's going to happen is you're going to create men without self-control. Men without self-control are not sitting at home eating ice cream, feeling depressed. They're rapists and they're murderers. They're psychopaths. They're serial killers. Because we have a biological programming. And you're going to tell men they can't control their urges. Don't control your urges. Don't suppress your emotions. If you feel like running that guy over, you just get in your car and you just run him over. It's garbage.

They think turning men into women is going to create a bunch of crybabies, and it will. But the opposite to a crybaby, the other end of the spectrum is a violent psychopath. And that's why all these school shootings and such are always some weirdo incel dude crying his eyes out. Next minute he turns up with an AK.

How is that beneficial to society as a whole? Men need to be told to control themselves, control their emotions, honour, valour, courage, self-discipline. All the old-school masculine traits are the only thing that keeps society together, because it's the only thing that even built society in the first place.

Now I need a drink. A gin and tonic. I've upset myself.

Paul: You know, it's not this clichéd view of masculinity where it's some idiot meathead who's got nothing to say for himself, who's got no prospects, and who just spends 12 hours in a gym every day.

But the fact is the bad boy image, it's not being a bad boy, it's having self-respect. That is the modern bad boy. Now that's what it's got down to. It's basically just having self-respect. Okay, no women are going to be attracted to you if you don't have your own interest, your own level of self-respect that doesn't revolve around chasing them. This is just basic, right?

Andrew: It's self-respect and it's sticking up for yourself and it's believing in something. You got to have something to believe in. You've got to be viable for standing up for something.

The truth is this: Every time a man is needed, there's emotional control involved. You're telling me a firefighter when he runs into a burning building isn't suppressing his fear? That's what makes him valuable: the fact that he's learned to suppress his fear and he's doing it anyway for the good of society. Same with the soldier, same with the policemen, same with everyone these liberals are going to call when shit hits the fan.

Paul: Which is why men need to suppress their emotions, which we're going to talk about with the depression thing; it's not always good to externalise your emotions as a man. In fact, most of the time it's terrible to do that, right?

Andrew: Well, absolutely. Man look, I've had 85 professional fights and I'll tell you now I was scared before every single fucking one. I've seen five men die in the ring. I put a guy in a wheelchair for life. I know what can happen. I am scared. Do I show it? No. Because how is it going to benefit me? It's going to give my enemy confidence.

And let's forget professional fighting. If you're walking down the street with your wife, three guys come up to take her handbag, you say "You know what, step away from her now", and you mean what you say. You can save her life without even throwing a punch. Instead of going "Oh well, I feel scared now guys, I'm really intimidated, please don't take her bag", kind of garbage. It's just absolute privilege. We talk about all these imaginary privileges. They pretend that being white is a privilege, they pretend being a man is a privilege, all this garbage.

The real privilege is living in a first world country where you can sit around with so few problems that you can invent issues like men being men and cry about it all day. That's a privilege. Garbage!

Paul: Let's get into that now because we've come on to it. I call it the depression industrial complex.

I made a video called "The age of emotional incontinence". And it's not just a big-pharma conspiracy to pathologise everything. Although that is going on in order to make billions of dollars from drug profits. But it's also this kind of global obsession pushed by the media, pushed by the culture, that we need to be emotionally incontinent so that we constantly need to talk about our feelings and cry all the time.

The old stiff upper lip thing, the British cliché, was generally true because people did grieve, they did mourn, but they did it privately. Because again to externalise everything and to have that constant track of victimhood rolling in your brain 24/7 is not going to lift you out of that situation.

We're told also that there's a stigma around depression. There's no stigma around depression. People bang on about it constantly on social media, on television. And the more they talk about it in many cases, the more depressed they become.

It's like when they introduced death education into schools and suicide skyrocketed. The more information that became available about the means to commit suicide, the more that suicide skyrocketed in the West.

You know, people seem to think that just telling them to pull themselves up by the bootstraps, is just a cliché. It's not a cliché. It's an entire branch of philosophy called stoicism. You can read about it. This isn't some basic bitch fridge-magnet philosophy. This is stoicism. This has been around for thousands of years.

The point is, that life is suffering. As soon as you learn to accept that, as soon as you learn to stop wallowing in your own circumstances, life becomes a bit easier, you become mentally stronger, and you're better at dealing with it. And that's the message you put across right, Andrew, and you got crucified for it.

Andrew: I got crucified. But this is what was so great like we said at the beginning.

Paul, I want to promise you from the bottom of my heart, I never for a single solitary second considered retracting my words ever. Because I meant what I said. And with a million retweets and every Hollywood celebrity in the world coming at me saying they can't wait till I apologise, I sat there with a smile on my face because I'm right.

Here's the reality of the world. Ying and Yang, old Chinese philosophy, joy and pain, light and dark, there is no up without down. There's no such thing as permanent happiness, because then it's not happiness, is it? You only feel happiness because you felt sad. You need the polarity to even experience it. This is what people don't understand.

People are going through life going "I deserve to be happy all the time". You're not a child who got a toy at Christmas. You're a grown-up. You've got responsibilities. You have things you need to do. You have pressure. You have commitments to fulfil. You're not going to be permanently happy all of the time. There's going to be times you feel a bit pissed off.

There's two types of people. The people who pull themselves up by the bootstraps like you said, who think "Well, I'm unhappy about my current situation so what I'm going to do is change it". Or the people who go "I'm unhappy, it's not my fault. I caught a disease. I'm depressed. Oh, no wonder I'm fat, I live in my mother's basement. I'm depressed". No. It's just complete garbage and people use it as an excuse for things.

I hear it all the time. People message me and go, "I'm overweight, what do I do?" I say "Go to the gym". They say, "I can't cause I'm depressed". I was like "You think you're fat because you're depressed, the reality is you're depressed because you're fat. You got it the wrong way around".

It's simply a situational feeling that's telling you you're unhappy with your situation, or you're unhappy with certain circumstances, and you need to change it. That's all it is. It's an evolutionary mechanism to prevent you living a life that humans are not meant to live.

If depression wasn't situational, why do people not like going to jail? Because when you go to jail, you're in a situation which is depressing, just as simple as that. If we can be happy all the time regardless, then how come we don't just all go commit a crime, sit in a jail cell, and get three meals a day?

And also, how come if this is a universal disease, does it have country borders? Certain countries are more depressed than others. Why does it stop at a country? Surely, it affects all the human race the same. No. Certain countries tell you to get over it and get on with your life. And certain countries molly-coddle you.

And when you're talking about the stigma, I come on Twitter and say openly I have sex with multiple women. I have three girlfriends and a bunch of other chicks and I get attacked. But If I come on to say I'm depressed, everyone's on my side. If I say I'm a heterosexual male, then I'm the enemy...

Paul: No, you can't say that. How dare you. You're happy and you're heterosexual, and you're enjoying life. My God!

Andrew: Absolutely insane. The only reason anyone's alive to hear this is because at some point in history a man had sex with a woman. And now I'm doing the same thing and I'm evil? But if I want to talk about being depressed, and that all white men should die, that's perfectly acceptable.

We want to talk about stigmas. There's stigmas attached to everything wrong in this life. There's absolutely no stigma around depression. Maybe if you're a soldier you have PTSD and it's called that for a reason because it's a different condition, or maybe like 0.1% of people genuinely have something wrong with them. Most people just need to be told to get up and get over it.

Man, when I was 16, because I was a kid and I was stupid, I was miserable about some shit. And I remember saying to my dad, "Oh, I think I'm depressed". I remember him saying to me, "Depression isn't real, go to the gym". And literally, within a day I was fixed. Because I went to the gym, I started training, I never thought about it again.

Imagine if he'd said "Oh my God, okay, let's take you to the doctor, let's take you to the therapist, let's talk about depression all the time, let's start taking these pills". No! These pills are going to alter your brain, and you sit there and talk about everything bad that's ever happened to you with this therapist.

Do you think I would have been cured in a day? Or would I have been been suffering from this imaginary garbage for years?

Paul: And the other the other thing is, Andrew, people do it for attention.

With the rise of social media, you've seen the 10 paragraph, 20 paragraph Facebook post with people whining about how depressed they are. They want attention. They're narcissists. It's not just people justifying their laziness. It's also people believing that because their friend got some attention on social media for something else, maybe for doing something actually productive and creative, then they get jealous.

You have this thing where people are scrolling through other people's Instagram feeds seeing that they're having fun, even though it's just a highlights reel of their life. Then they get depressed about that. So they think oh, how can I draw attention to myself?

And I've known people recently who just described themselves "Oh, I'm autistic, I've got disassociative disorder" or some bullshit, some anomalous bullshit, simply to make themselves feel special so they can then go around their little social group and on social media saying "This is wrong with me, I'm a victim, give me attention". That's a big part of it as well, isn't it?

Andrew: Of course, it is. It's an instant path to uniqueness.

I mean, for you personally to be unique, you have created some of the most interesting political commentary of our time. For me to be unique, I have to go and train and break bones and be a professional fighter. But these people want to be unique and they go "Oh, yeah, but you don't understand what it's like to live with OCD". OCD... Shut up! There's nothing wrong with you.

You know what, I was watching TV with one of my ex-girlfriends a few years ago, and there was a kid on there who had OCD. And this kid had to walk down the stairs in a certain order. He had like skipped one and then jumped two and then go back up, whatever. And the parents were saying if Timmy doesn't do the stairs in the right order, then Timmy gets really upset and he has panic attacks.

And I was sitting with this girl saying "This is invented and they're facilitating it. They're enabling him and telling him, saying it's okay for him to throw a tantrum. It's imaginary".

And she goes to me "Well, how do you know it's imaginary?" And I said "Have you ever seen a kid in Africa walk four miles for water twice because they missed a step?" No. Because it's not real. None of it's real, it's called enabling and facilitating.

Talk about a stigma. The only stigma around depression is telling someone there's nothing wrong with their life and to grow up.

Paul: That's the only stigma, that's the only thing you'll get crucified for.

And yeah, people do it to feel special. They've always got nothing else going on in their lives. They've got some shit dead end job that doesn't fulfil them at all, that doesn't give them any creative purpose or fulfilment. So they say "Oh, I'm autistic, I've got this disorder, that disorder". No, your life is shit, you need to improve it. Stop wallowing. Stop whining.

Yeah, we all get down from time to time. But once you get over the hump of those situations, then stuff gets better and it's called stoicism.

Read some Seneca. Read some books on stoicism, they will help you. Whining about it, wallowing about it every day on social media, making excuses for your own shit life, you're never going to fix it, you're never going to solve it.

Andrew: Depression is the number one thing. But in general, the problem that plagues modern society in the West, is that every single person wants to absolve responsibility. What they want to do is say "This situation that I'm in is shit, but it's not my fault. It's politics fault". Or I'm fat because of my thyroid. Or I'm depressed. Or I've got OCD. Even people who are alcoholics or drug addicts are still trying to blame something else.

You got up, you got dressed, you went to the store, you got a fiver out of your pocket, you bought booze, you walked home with the booze, and you drank the booze. And who else are you blaming?

Is there not any point in that process where you paused and thought maybe you should stop drinking booze? And you want to say you have a disease? I mean this is all just absolving responsibility.

I said this to someone the other day. I said if I can go through that process of buying alcohol and be an alcoholic, surely, everything bad you do, every shit life decision you make can be a disease? Why can't I just go start stealing stuff and claim I can't control myself, I have a disease and I can't help it? Anything to take responsibility away from myself.

And depression is the cure-all. With depression, you have an excuse for being unhealthy, out of shape, bad job, no motivation. Anything you can think of that's negative, you can go ah, I'm depressed, yes. It's just a perfect excuse. That's all it is, is an excuse. And it's insane that people enable it.

When someone says they're depressed, everyone huddles around them and goes, poor you, poor you, and it just makes them worse. It's stupid.

Paul: And again, the more we talk about it, the more depression and suicide increases in the West, for both men and women. So whatever people are doing, it's not working.

So now, let's talk about pussy-hyperinflation because this is something else I've noticed.

Good-looking men, and I know some of these people, they're tall, confident, intelligent, good-looking guys, are hanging around with fives and sixes.

And not just fucking them, but professing love for them and shit. It's getting quite weird out there. We had an OK Cupid dating site release of some statistics which revealed that women found 80% of men to be less than average in attractiveness. Bearing in mind, half of these women are going to be quite ugly themselves.

On Tinder, the bottom 80% of men in terms of attractiveness are competing for the bottom 22% of women, and the top 78% of women are competing for the top 20% of men. So, men seem to be settling for uglier and uglier women. Why?

Andrew: Well firstly I'd like to apologise to men as a whole for what I've done.

Paul: It's all you. You're taking care of that 78% of women.

Andrew: Well, you know, bro, you know I stay busy.

So the problem is this: There's too much thirst, that's the issue. Typically, in the olden days, men gave attention to a woman to get sex, and the woman gave her sex back to keep getting the man's attention. That was the exchange: attention, sex; sex, attention, vice versa.

Now we live in a world where women get attention for just existing. You can be basic. If you put a picture on Instagram, you're going to get a bunch of likes from a bunch of dudes. Your inbox is going to be filled.

So, male attention no longer has value. So what does a man have to give to get girls? Usually, in the old days a man gave his attention to get girls, but that no longer works. So now what works?

Well, either you're a super high value male where your attention is super valuable. Like famous. Or you have a bunch of money. And that's what the top 20% is.

In many cases, those two things, the money and fame, go together if you're a celebrity, or a famous athlete or something.

But that's what's happening. So now women are sitting around thinking "Okay, well, I get my basic dudes all day. I want something special".

They themselves aren't special, but they still believe they deserve it. So if you're a normal dude living a normal life, you're stuck with the fucking scraggles. And now it's all messed up.

I actually have a course on my website where I teach men how to get girls. And the first thing I teach them is you need to re-attach value to your attention. Because attention has no value. You need to do something to weaponise your attention again to get her to interact with you, or you don't stand a chance.

And that's what I teach. And that's how I got all these guys hitting me up saying wow, you changed my life, blah, blah. But that's what basically has happened in the western world, and it's a complete mess, man.

I don't know how most of these guys out here are surviving. It's horrible. And that's how you give rise to all these webcam companies and all this E-Thot stuff. Because you've got basic dudes sitting at home, desperate and lonely, and this is where it all comes from.

Paul: The issue with the E-Thot thing is a lot of these women who sit on Twitch with their tits hanging out, begging for money, well not even begging for money, they don't even have to ask for it anymore, they just sit there and it rolls in minute after minute from incels. They're getting the money but they're not even that attractive.

Mostly they're just sixes with big ample breasts, and actually saggy breasts in many cases, but they wear the push-up bra, and the money just rolls in.

Some of them are even preaching Trad-Life shit which makes it even more hilarious.

But as you said, you've got girls across social media, some of them don't even sit on camera. They've just got Instagram pages, a Patreon link to it, they're making hundreds of thousands of dollars a month just for dressing up in cosplay and making themselves look slutty.

You know, do we blame the girls or do we blame the incels? What does it say about the state of manhood in today's society that men are just throwing away their resources because some six on Twitch might DM them once a week? How pathetic is that?

Andrew: You know why I'm laughing? Because you are absolutely correct. One of my businesses, I have a few, one of them I've kind of retired from the industry. But for a long time, I had a webcam studio. So I know this business inside out. Big misogynist Andrew had 75 girls working for him, oh, no.

Paul: You were paying women thousands of dollars a month. The horror! Giving them careers oh, my God. Such a sexist!

Andrew: They're not all beauty queens, though. They're just approachable and friendly. And there's dudes out there who will spend money just for a woman to talk to them. You know what I find a lot of the time? It's not just the lonely virgins, but often it's the dude who's in a sexless marriage, afraid of divorce because of the laws.

His kids don't respect him, his wife hates him, and he waits for everyone to go to sleep and logs into his little computer, telling the girl "I love you, baby; baby, I really love you. I love you".

It's the truth because they want the attention. People go "Oh, why don't they get a hooker?" They don't want sex, they want attention from a female.

And if a woman has a good personality, I said this all the time when I was hiring girls, it doesn't matter what you look like.

If you're friendly, if you have good banter, and you're a good person, you're going to do well. And that's what it is. These girls are not exceptionally hot.

And you can't blame the girls. The girls will sit there, talk shit, and make more money than a judge. I mean, are you going to tell them not to? It's insane. Male thirst is so out of control that women profit from it insanely. And it's all over the internet.

So when this whole E-Thot shaming and all these things went down, it was attacking the girls. She's a whore, she's a whore.

I have girls who worked for me who were married at 18, with one man in their life. Had a kid young, trad-life, literally genuinely trad-life girls, but they're just making so much easy money. They're like "They can call me a whore, but I know I'm not", and these guys are just sending them money for nothing. Can you blame the chicks? I don't blame the chicks at all.

Paul: Yeah. And people wonder why guys watch babe station and other TV channels of these girls writhing around on beds. Not even naked in many cases, just writhing around. It's barely even soft porn when they've got all the free hardcore porn at their fingertips.

And it's exactly what you said. They need the connection. They need the conversation from a woman because they're not getting it in their own marriages, their own relationships. That's what's sad about it.

Also, I knew this cam girl who actually I'm going to try and get on the channel, and she said that most of the guys who want to chat to her, their fantasy is not even to have her talking about banging them. Instead it's to have her talking about banging somebody else. In many cases a black guy, and it's a cuck fantasy. And she said it was literally like 75-80% of the calls she got were men wanting her to talk about that.

So again, that comes back to this complete wrecking of confidence, wrecking of manhood, wrecking of masculinity, but that's what they want to talk about, right?

Andrew: Absolutely. And I think a lot of fetishes are born of frustration. I mean I'll tell you something now, and maybe it's too much information but whatever. I have so many beautiful women and I'm not into anything weird. I don't need to be into anything weird.

I have beautiful girls, I enjoy pretty much normal dominant sex with my beautiful women. If all you get is ugly chicks, or you never have sex at all, then your mind's going to warp and you're going to end up into something weird.

Every single one of these dudes is into being a cuck, licking feet, being insulted. We used to have guys go on there, I don't know who they were because they hide their faces, but they'd have like a Kuwaiti IP address. And they're obviously millionaires because they were sending $10,000 a week, and they'd be like "Tell me you'll never had sex with a Muslim guy, tell me I'm stupid", because they're so dominant in their own hierarchy.

Paul: Exactly. I knew this other girl who straight up told me they wanted her to piss on the Quran, that was what they were into.

Andrew: Yeah, loads of Muslims are into having Islam insulted. So it's just sexual frustration.

Frustration ends up in some weird fetish, so the whole place is full of fetishes because you're full of sexually frustrated dudes. It's insane. So yeah, the cuck fetish is a huge thing.

The world is messed up and it's messed up on a level you wouldn't believe. What's scary about it is this: These were like doctors, lawyers, people you trust. There's people you're supposed to trust in society on these sites. I saw it with my own eyes. Because thirst is biological. Men are evolutionarily programmed. We're programmed to want a certain thing.

And the price of it is so exorbitant now for even the most basic version. The most basic version of pussy, is so badly over-priced. The guys just give up and think: you know what, this girl likes me, I'll just send her some money, and I'll just jack off. And that's just literally how it goes, it's crazy.

Paul: Now, female friends. I know you've talked about this before. There's a famous video on YouTube, I don't know if you've seen it, where this guy I think he's walking around at college, he asks about a dozen men and a dozen women, can men and women just be friends? All the women say yeah, of course, no problem whatsoever. All the guys say no, because when they're honest, they don't just want to be friends, they want to bang them.

Basically, unless the relationship is professional, unless there's a real practical reason for having to be in close contact with a woman, and tell me if I'm right, I'm guessing which way you're going to go on this... as a man you will get fucked up, and they will fuck you up on a regular basis if you have female friends.

Unless it's professional as a man, you can't have female friends, right?

Andrew: Absolutely. There's one really important point I forgot, bro, about the last subject. And that is, I'm sorry, I have to drop this in.

One of my number one cam girls polled all her dudes on who was pro-Trump, and who's anti-Trump. And there was like three pro-Trump guys and four hundred Democrats. So I just want to point that out. It's the people who are so feminist, and pro-feminism, they're the people who end up jacking off on the web...

So no, I don't have female friends, and I completely agree with you, because I don't see the benefit.

We live in a culture now where everyone's seen the Friends TV show, and we pretend that men and women have so much in common. We all want to sit around and talk about the same things. I have never listened to two women talking and thought "That's so interesting, oh wow, yeah, I use Pantene also". I'm not interested in what they care about, and they're not interested in what I care about.

My relationships with females are purely sexual or purely professional. I cannot see myself going "Oh, we're just friends let's just hang out". I don't see the benefit to it. On top of that, in my video, I made a point that women aren't combat ready

And the reason I said that was this. I'll tell you a quick story.

I was in a kebab shop about five years ago in Luton. This car pulled up, it was a blacked out Audi, and these four big black dudes got out. They walked straight to the front of the queue, pushing in front of everyone and just started ordering.

And there's a guy who was there was with this girl. And the girl goes "Hey, there's a queue". And as a professional fighter, I knew it was trouble. So I just thought "Why give a shit? Some people just aren't worth fucking with. There's four of them.

So she goes "Oh, oh, there's a queue", and one of them turns around and he says "Tell your girlfriend to shut up". And the guy goes "She's not my girlfriend, she's my friend".

So even then I thought you're about to get your ass kicked. You don't even get the pussy, and she's running her mouth.

Anyway she talked too fresh and the dude got knocked out clean in front of me. And I thought "You're hanging around with this mouthy chick who's your friend, who can't even fight, and you just got your ass whooped".

This is why when I say women aren't combat ready, it's the truth. If I'm walking with men and something goes down, or someone attacks me, you have brothers with you who can help you. Women are just useless in most situations, they're useless in combat situations, they're useless in any kind of physical situation.

But they want to walk around, take all my attention, expect me to buy them drinks and buy them dinner, and then not have sex with me, and call me their friend. I don't see the benefits in any of them.

Paul: The other thing which is even worse, when you make the mistake of making a female friend and you don't want to bang them because they're quite ugly. But they've got a thing about you and you're not interested, or you've got a girlfriend; that's when they will fuck you up.

Because your bros have your back, okay. They don't fuck you over behind the scenes. When you've got a female friend, her loyalty is not to you, it's to her other sisters. So she will talk shit about you, she will try and fuck up your life. That's why it's not worth it.

Andrew: Oh, absolutely. Girl Power! "I thought she deserved to know". You're completely right. Women love attention. They absolutely know they love attention and they love getting their own way.

There's two dynamics. Because the one you describe, where the female likes you, you don't like her back, then she tries to

destroy your relationship. Or the guy likes the girl, the girl
doesn't like the guy, the girl pretends she's unaware that the
dude's obviously in love with her, pretends oh, we're just
friends, I've known him since school. Yeah, he buys me
Christmas presents and pays for my dinners, but we're just
friends.

It's just pathetic naivety, and it's put on, and it's not real. I
don't need female friends. I don't need them.

Paul: There's a famous Facebook post, and it's a picture of a
man and a woman. The man posts "We look like a couple
here", and then the woman responds below "Yeah, a couple of
besties." He got friend-zoned hard in there.

Let's move on to a not so similar subject. Islam.

Now, Mike Cernovich got a lot of heat for this tweet a few
days ago. He said "Christianity has given us a country where 11
year olds dance for adult men who throw dollars on the stage".
This was talking about drag queen kids. "Christianity gave us a
church that molested children and sold out their flock to the
left. A moderated form of Islam is probably the West's only
hope".

Quite the leap to go from drag queen kids to a moderated
form of Islam for the West. From my perspective that's some-
what bullshit because there's no such thing as moderate Islam.

You know, 50% of moderate Muslims in the UK want to lock
up gay people in cages. Massive numbers of them support
suicide bombings in certain circumstances.

These are the moderate Muslims. it was moderate Muslims
that hid Abdeslam, the Paris massacre terrorist for three
months in Malambique while the police were looking for him.

Malaysia is the most moderate Islamic country on earth, yet
it's rife with anti-Semitism. There's no such thing as moderate
Islam.

But we have this problem in the West where we've got this nihilistic meaningless culture. We've got community cohesion and family bonds weakening by the year. We have nothing to believe in for young people. Islam provides young people something to believe in. It provides people with that strong community and family bonds.

So you can understand why some people even on the Right see it as preferable to this hedonistic, nihilistic meaningless lifestyle which offers nothing. Especially to young people who just fall into this cycle of degeneracy.

You told a story on one of your videos where you went into a nightclub with a Muslim friend, and his view of women. Tell us what he told you about the women in that nightclub and how that relates to Islam in the West.

Andrew: The thing about Islam is this, and I'll tell you the truth. Islam has won.

In Western Europe, I believe Islam has won. I believe the fight is over.

You cannot criticise them. They have strong community and they believe in their faith above everything else. They don't care about country borders. They don't care about colour. All they care about is their faith.

On top of that, they're going to out-breed us anyway. They're having children young. We don't have children. It's like this is on every level.

I live currently in Romania which is overtly orthodox Christian. And still to this day if I go on a date with a 22-year-old woman, she'll say she has to be home at ten. Her Dad said so.

So I live in a country where family bond and religion still exists.

And then when I go back to England, I can see exactly how much it doesn't exist. Because you see a 17-year-old throwing up on the pavement because she had too many pints trying to keep up with her mates. So everything you said is completely correct. We have created a cultural void...

Paul: Which is not saying we want them to cover up and that we want a modesty culture. Surely, there's a middle ground there, right?

Andrew: Absolutely there needs to be a middle ground. I don't know if Mike's point was the same as mine, but I'm pessimistic about the future. I think that especially in Europe, the fight's over.

I really genuinely believe that. I should be saying we'll resist, and we will resist. But just by pure numbers and the fact that they're so dedicated to their faith. Nobody in the West is dedicated to anything.

Besides people like you and me who genuinely stick our necks out, and are persecuted, there's no-one.

We cannot get a job and we're not hireable. Look at all the stuff we have to go through just to say half of the truth. Most people just shut up and be quiet. They're not dedicated to anything. That's the end. That's the end of the whole situation in my view.

Plus on top of all of this, not only does Islam provide a sense of identity, but you want to tie it to what we were saying earlier, Islam provides women.

This is what the Muslim friend I went to the club with said: "Here in England you can find girls to sleep with, but you can't find a wife". I said "What do you mean?" And he points to these two girls dancing with each other sexually in the dance floor. "Would you marry her?"

And I looked at them close, and he had a point. Under Islam, even if you're a baker, even if you're broke, even if you have nothing, if you're all of those things, you'll still get a wife and she'll still listen to you, and she'll still have your kids, and she'll still cook you dinner.

Now that's reason enough for a whole bunch of people to not give up their religion. That's reason enough...

Paul: So what you're saying is incels should convert to Islam?

Andrew: If you've got Islam, what have you got? Well, at the moment I'm just a nobody. But under Islam at least I have a wife. So there's a whole bunch of tenets to Islam which makes it such a powerful force, and that's why it's so dangerous.

Christianity is losing its grip. America is still a religious country. But in Western Europe, Christianity has no serious power in anything, in any realm.

I'm an atheist, and as an atheist I still say I love living in a country that refuses to build mosques because it's a Christian country and they only build churches.

I respect that because the country is built on Christian traditions. England needs to come along and say "We were built on Christian traditions, regardless of whether we still believe or not. This is a Christian country, Christian traditions, we're not building anything else". And I don't think there's anything wrong with saying that. Because we certainly can't build churches in their countries.

I don't hate on Islam, I want to get that very clear. I'm not racist in any way. My view of the world is an ultra-realistic view that the weak get conquered and the strong survive. And the world has always been that way.

Paul: And they have stronger tribes. Our society is atomised to the point where we don't even talk to our neighbours.

I walked past my immediate neighbour the other day, said hello, and he looked at me like I was insane. And I mean, I know this is London, but come on! Maybe he's found out who I am, maybe some other reason.

Andrew: This is exactly the point, you said it perfectly. We're completely atomised.

And this is the thing that's dangerous, and it's dangerous on every level. Because when you talk about weak versus strong, no one can be strong on their own. We're only strong as a unifying force. We can't even unify under a flag anymore because the flag is racist. We can't unify under anything.

So you're left with these people who believe in the art of conquest. People often say that America belongs to the native Americans... Well, not really because they lost the fight. You can't go through the world and say well, they were here first, so it's theirs. Not really, if you lose the fight.

Paul: They were killing each other in their own tribes long before the Europeans ever showed up.

Andrew: And every country border on earth, basically every single one has been defined by war. Someone won something, someone lost something, and the border was drawn.

So conquest is a real right to land. So my view on the world is the weak will perish and and the strong survive.

If Western Europe as a society is so weak that they're going to allow people in unlimited numbers to turn up and kill us, people who'll do anything to protect their ideology, well then we're going to get destroyed.

And am I mad at the people destroying us? No. The strong are always going to defeat the weak. So to me, it's just kind of like well, we've walked into it, that's my view.

Paul: I mean we had a story the other day about a comedian on the BBC called Russell Howard, who is like the most safe, unfunny, woke comedian you could ever imagine. He wanted to make a joke about ISIS after the Charlie Hebdo attacks. And the BBC told him he would have to re-script that because they didn't want to offend Islamic State. That's how bad it's got in the United Kingdom. We could go on for ages about that.

Also, you've got progressives traveling to these Islamic countries, thinking that the world is a Utopia, projecting their Utopian malaise onto other countries, and they end up getting beheaded, they end up getting raped, they end up getting strangled to death. I've made videos about this.

We also have another breed of basic-bitch travelers who go to these shit-hole countries trying to chase some authentic cultural experience. Just so they could come back and tell their friends how culturally enriched they are.

But they're literally going to places like New Delhi where they have to do UN training programs telling the population not to shit on the streets because it causes childhood diseases which kills thousands of children.

Andrew: Bro, these people are dangerous. They're either dangerous to themselves or they're dangerous to society. Because here's what they do. They live in a warped dimension where negative stereotypes about a country are invented.

Paul, you horrible right-wing individual, and me Mr. Fucking Terrible, we've invented all these stereotypes to all these countries, we just made it up. We've made it up because we're racist.

And they think that if you go there, it's actually perfectly safe. And then one of two things unfolds. Either something terrible happens to them and they have to learn the hard way. And unfortunately, in these kind of societies, they'd rather just kill you than let you go to the police.

So in 99% of cases they end up dead. Or by some miracle they manage to survive and then they come back and they're even worse. "Well, I went to Afghanistan and actually, the people were lovely". What do you mean they're lovely? There's land mines. There's IEDs.

Paul: Even in that story where they got killed. They got mowed down by ISIS in Tajikistan, that bicycling couple who said "Oh, our view of the world is backwards, you know, there're other certainly more dangerous countries, it's just a reflection of their own bigotry" and all this crap they put on their blog.

I read their blog. And in almost every Islamic country they visited before they got killed, they were harassed, they were stalked, they were robbed, they were physically assaulted.

So again, it's not as if they didn't have any warnings. They ended up getting mowed down, and stabbed to death by ISIS.

So many other examples like that. Obviously most people aren't going to get killed, aren't going to get raped if they go to Morocco or whatever.

So it's the ones who go not so far afield, they stay within tourist bubbles and come back and say "Oh no, it's really great, I don't know what you're talking about". As soon as you go outside the bubble, you're in trouble.

Andrew: Well, absolutely. Look, let's just stick to some realities of life. I don't like to call myself a sexist. I don't like to call myself a racist. I'm none of those things. I'm a realist.

Certain parts of the world are more dangerous than others. I can walk down the street here in Romania with my blonde girlfriend in a skirt and nothing's bad is going to happen, but in many parts of the world I cannot do that. And I understand that. That doesn't make me a racist, doesn't make me a psycho.

But when you say that to people, they're like "Oh, well, have you even ever been there?" As if I should try it out first and walk through Baghdad with a Playboy bunny to prove i'm right.

Paul: You've been to Iraq anyway, right?

Andrew: I have been to Iraq. I was in Iraq actually for some work. And you know what was surprising about Iraq? It was not as interesting as I expected to be. But it was filled with Chinese people.

The Chinese are just rebuilding the whole place. It's crazy that America spends money bombing it to hell, and the Chinese people have all got construction contracts. Getting all the money rebuilding. I could have been in Beijing there were so many Chinese there.

But yeah, many parts of the world are not safe and that's perfectly normal. I mean I've traveled the world, around 72 countries. A lot of people pretend traveling teaches you something. I actually disagree with that completely.

A lot of people say "Oh, but when you travel, you learn about yourself". What they're really saying is "I live in my parent's house, I have an allowance account, and this is the first time in my life I had to do my own laundry". That's all. It is basic responsibility for finding somewhere to sleep, and finding a way to clean your shirts. Like you don't learn anything travelling.

Paul: Well, it's the old adage about going away to find yourself, and you just find out that you're still an idiot.

They go to like Thailand and claim it's such an amazing experience, just to come back and lord it over their friends, like they've experienced something out of this world. Like they've gone to Jupiter or something.

Everything's been done in terms of travel, unless you're going to go to the Moroccan hinterlands and get beheaded. I don't think anyone wants to do that.

But their little Instagram selfie has been done by like a

billion other people. Yeah, you can go on holiday and have fun. That's great.

But don't come back and say that you went through this magical experience, because it's bullshit, right?

Andrew: You get it all the time.

I lived in Thailand for two years when I was fighting. And you had people there genuinely trying to pretend they're lost. Pretending they just found a waterfall when they actually paid to go there with a load of other tourists. But on their Instagram they apparently "found it". You know, it's such manufactured garbage.

I met a dude with long hair and I was talking to him. He was saying "Oh, I started growing my hair when I came to Thailand". I was like "Why?", "Oh, you know, when i'm traveling, it's hard to get a cut". And my brother said "There's a barbershop over there... "

Paul: That's because he wants to come back and have it as part of his image that he went through this spiritual transformation, right?

Andrew: They think they're Robinson Crusoe but still in the number one tourist destination on Earth. Like what planet are you on? People can take it even farther like you said and end up in Tajikistan to be able to say well, I actually went somewhere you've never been, but...

Paul: They got raped and beheaded, how progressive.

Let's leave it there for now.

So, Cobratate.com, tell people about the courses you're offering and why everyone should get them.

Andrew: Yeah, I learned a lot in the webcam industry. I've retired from that industry now but i've written courses.

I have courses on how to pick up women that are not in a horrible evil pick-up artists way. It's just what I've learned about girls, working with so many of them, what I've learned about men, especially the men who are paying them for attention, and how you can have a better relationship with females.

It doesn't matter if you're married, it doesn't matter if you're trying to find a wife, it doesn't matter if you're trying to be a playboy, or just had a bad relationship with females.

I've got a whole bunch of courses on there, with everything from chess to fitness, how to run webcam studio, body language, everything's all there. I'm proud of absolutely everything I produce, and I guarantee you it's some life-changing information. You can check it out, I think you'll be impressed.

VIOLENCE IS NECESSARY

Violence is the bottom line.

I read a really good article by a man called Jack Donovan. And his speech (I won't plagiarise it or try and impersonate it or do it justice), is called Violence is Golden.

You should be able to Google it and find it if you want to read his version of events. But basically, I was reading these words and nodding in agreement, and thinking that this has always been my mindset.

Have you ever had one of those situations where you've thought a certain way your whole life, and it seems nobody else really feels the same? Then, finally you see somebody else thinks the exact same thing. It might be written in a different way and explained in a different way, but it's the same. It was really interesting. It was one of those "Ah, I'm not the only one" moments.

What I'm talking about is violence, and how violence is a universal constant across humanity. Always has been, always will be. And how important violence is, and how violence is absolutely necessary. It's never going to disappear or go away, because violence is needed.

. . .

So I've had a saying for a long time.

My saying is "What are they going to do, fight me?" And I use it a lot.

My girlfriend catches me cheating? Well, what's she's going to do, fight me? Like, what were you going to do? The point is, unless someone's going to get violent with you, what other repercussions really are there? Everything else is just wishy-washy bullshit. Everything else is just talk, just words. If they're not going to put their hands on you, none of it's real. It's just talk. It's just garbage.

And it also demonstrates how unimportant the consequence of something is. Cheat on my girlfriend, what's she going to do do? Well, she might leave. She might cry. She might complain. She might...

But she isn't going to come up and stab me. Well, maybe she'll try, and if she does, I'm very prepared. Don't come at me with some knife spouting this fucking bimbo shit you see in the movies, "YOU CHEATED!!!" ... Fucking, get the fuck out of here, talking about cheating. Of course, I did.

Now put the knife down or use it to go make me a fucking sandwich.

I understand the reality of how violence is the final straw. Violence is the bottom line, violence is binary. We either get violent or we don't. If we don't, it doesn't matter; and if we do, let's get violent. All the talk, all that is garbage

And so Jack in his essay made a very, very good point.

Jack's point came out from a slightly different angle. His point was that everybody believes in violence. The biggest paci-fist in the world believes in violence. You reading this believes in violence. Everyone believes in violence. Except we live in a society where we've sanitised violence by allowing violence to be committed by other people for us.

Violence by proxy. We don't have to kill our own food anymore, they kill the food for us, so we don't have to see the violent part, we just get the meat.

And it's exactly the same with everything. If something happens and we need help, we call the police, and we expect the police to be capable of being violent if the need arises. We're not violent ourselves, but we'll call someone else to be violent for us.

Imagine I'm at your house and I got this fucking weapon, and you call the police. But when the police arrive they're not allowed to be violent. I could just kill everyone there.

Everyone believes in violence. We just believe in violence by proxy. Because without violence by proxy, there's no law; it doesn't matter what the law is. If there's not the underlying threat that violence will happen at some point, nobody will listen to anything.

The only reason we live in a society with so little violence is because the threat of violence constantly permeates through our society. The fact that people can be violent and the police and the state can be violent against you is the reason that things get solved in a non-violent way.

You give me a parking ticket, I don't want to pay. Fuck you, I don't pay. You add money to the fine, I don't pay.

You threaten me with another court date, I don't show up. You send someone around to ask why I didn't show up, I tell them to fuck off.

The police come and say "Look, you've taken the piss with this thing, you need to come to your next court date". No, fuck you, I don't. Then they arrest me.

When they try and arrest me and say "You're coming to the police station", I say "No, I don't want to come. I'm not coming".

Then what happens? They forcibly, violently grab me, put my hands behind my back, chain me up, and take me to a cell where I'm held against my will. From a parking ticket to violence, that's how it escalates.

Now why do people pay their parking ticket in the first place? Because they know that if they go down that chain of events, eventually, violence happens.

So the only reason we live in a non-violent society is people decide "You know what, I'll just pay the fine". They agree to non-violent resolutions because if they don't, they understand eventually there'll be a violent resolution. Violence is always the final answer. I'm not saying it's the best answer. I'm not saying the only answer. But it is the final answer.

It's the last answer, when reasoning fails, when being nice fails, when trying to intimidate people fails, when adding money on top of the fine fails, when talk fails, when all that shit fails.

It gets violent. That's the reality of the world and every single law we have, from parking tickets, to tax codes, to anything you can think of. Ultimately they are backed with a threat of violence.

So if you're going to sit here and deny what I'm saying, or pretend what I'm saying isn't true, then you're a moron.

It's very, very simple. You believe in violence when you need it. If you're a pussy, you get someone else to do it for you. My question is this. Do you trust the government? Do you trust other people to do violence for you better than you can? When someone breaks into your house, do you want someone else to use violence to protect you or do you use violence yourself?

I have an intimate relationship with violence because I was a professional fighter. But I've always understood how important violence is because it's never going anywhere and it's a universal constant that underpins our societies.

So I want to be good at violence, as should you. You should be good at the number one thing which is definitely going to exist forever.

The number one thing that is used to control who you are, where you go, how you think, and what you do, is a threat of violence.

You need to be comfortable with violence. I'm not saying that you have to be a violent person, but you need to be comfortable with it.

So, that's why fighting's so important, and that's why pacifists are full of shit.

~

THE BIGGEST MISTAKE MEN MAKE AS THEY GET OLDER

So i'm talking to some bitch. And she's asking me when am I ever going to grow up?

I'm like "Grow up?" I'm six foot three. I'm big and strong and rich. I got mansions. I got a supercar collection. People know my name. "What are you talking about? You're fucking 22. If you didn't have fat titties I wouldn't even be talking to you".

But she's like "Oh you know, you know, you just run around the world with your brother, just driving supercars, just being crazy. When are you going to, you know, grow up and settle down?"

Growing up and settling down are not the same thing.

Settling down is what happens when a man loses his lust for life. Settling down is for the man who thinks he's found the best he could possibly ever have. And that it's worth sacrificing all of the adventure in his existence to retain it. That's what settling down is. It has nothing to do with maturity, nothing to do with growing up.

I'm very grown up. I just don't want to sit with you and

watch fucking Netflix when I could drive super cars through the mountains with my brother.

I'd rather go down the mountain pass in my Mclaren 765LT with my brother than sit next to you watching bullshit.

That does not make me any less mature than a pussy-ass dude who's settled.

So she's sitting there going "Well, my friend's husband, when he got married he stopped blah, blah, blah". And this is a big problem with the world today.

It's low value men.

I tried to explain this to her and by the end of it she kind of understood and it broke her heart, because by the time she understood it, she realised that "Shit, my Disney fairy tale idea of finding the perfect man at the right time and him settling down isn't real".

Because perfect men never settle down, because perfect men don't have to settle down. If you're a low value man, you have to give everything about yourself to try and inspire loyalty from a female.

So no man wants to sit home and watch Netflix. No man wants to not roll with his boys. No man wants to be monogamous. No man wants to do these things.

But the only way he can try and hope his female is loyal to him, is if he's with her every day and he doesn't cheat and he pretends to enjoy the trips to IKEA on the weekend on his only day off. "Hmm, yeah, I think those curtains, yeah, maybe well they're yellow and the couch is yellow". No man wants that.

But for a very low value man, the only way you can possibly hope that the chick you're with doesn't end up getting fucked by me is to sit there and do all that shit.

That's what you have to do, because you want your female to be loyal. Every man out there knows they want their female to be loyal. It's a biological evolutionary hard-wired trait of masculinity that you want your female to be loyal to only you.

Look at the Islamic world, or look at the third world. Females get in big trouble for not being loyal. Every man wants a loyal female, right? So low value men have to give up basically their entire existence to inspire loyalty from a female.

And what I was trying to explain to her is this - I don't have to do that. You've been loyal to me for three years. I see you once a month. You cry over me every night. I ain't fucking taking you anywhere. I ain't missed a single day of having fun. I haven't grown up for 10 seconds to keep your ass. Do you know why?

Because I'm a big G. Because there's no other kickboxing world-champion athlete, retired, multi-millionaire with diamond watches and fucking supercars running around like me.

If you're not fucking me, it's a downgrade. You know it and I know it. So you have a choice. You either get once a month with the Ferrari, or every day with the Nissan. You chose the Ferrari.

That's what you decided to do. That's why you'll never cheat on me. That's why you'll be loyal to me because you're not going to let some loser come and fuck you. Every other man's a loser. True or false? She's like "Well, yeah, compared to you they are, but... "

No, but.

You've been fucked by the boss, you're not going to be fucked by them. I don't even have to try and make you be loyal. You have enough of a brain to look at me and realise anyone after me is nothing but a downgrade. There's nowhere for you to go, bitch.

So with that in mind, why the fuck am I going to give up my life when I can get your loyalty anyway?

The only kind of girl who I can't get instant loyalty from is a complete whore. And guess what? A complete whore, even if I gave up everything for her would eventually continue down the path of being a complete whore, because whores are whores.

But good women, when they meet a man like me, they're loyal because there's nowhere else to go.

So I have no reason to settle down or "grow up". I enjoy my life. I enjoy freedom. And when every other man out here has a wife going "Oh well, maybe you should be home because it's the kid's birthday... and Jerry and Jane are coming over and I've cooked meatloaf..."

Meanwhile I'm in Dubai surrounded by bitches, and they're going to sit there and look at my life and go "Oh, he just hasn't grown up yet".

And if you were a fraction of the man I am today, you wouldn't be sitting at home watching fucking Netflix pretending you're happy with it. Because you're not. It's a coping mechanism.

Men desire adventure. Why since the dawn of human time did men get in fucking armies and walk in random directions looking for someone to kill? Because this is how we are inside of us. We want adventure deep inside of us.

But the modern world is trying to squash it out of us, destroy the masculine essence, destroy the adventurous essence. Make us into little tax slaves who are afraid of our lives and sit at home and pretend they're mature. They sit at home and get one blow job a month. You fell for a trick.

So I told this bitch, that's the low value men. Real men like me, we don't have to do that, because I have no advantage to doing that.

I will never give up my life. And if you're a man reading this and you have given up your life, I want you to take a long hard look in the mirror. Look at the man staring back at you and ask yourself, are you really happy, or would you be happier living a life of adventure? Because we both know what the answer is.

One more point. I argue this subject with "grown up" men all the time.

And I tell them "Listen, you bitch, if you could press a

button, and your wife would be loyal for eternity, wait for you at home and never complain or nag, don't tell me you'd be home".

You would press that button. You'd come home, get a blow job, and you'd go off kite surfing. So who are you lying to? You're lying to me or you're lying to yourself? Bullshit.

At the end of this conversation, this girl's all upset and shit. "So well....., you're always just going to have all these girls?"

Yes. So fuck her.

PROMOTION OF FEMININITY

The reason femininity is so promoted is because it's a direct competitor to masculinity.

And the reason masculinity is directly attacked is very simple:

Every single rebellion and revolution in history took place when men got pissed off and went to the streets. If you're the elites of the world, and there's only a few of you, and a lot of very pissed-off men, you have to make sure these men don't realise - "I'm working for fucking nothing, they've forced me to put a mask on, they've closed my business, they've taken my travel away".

If you want to do something like the coronavirus then you have to destroy masculinity absolutely.

And you do that by taking one man, putting him with one woman, make it basically impossible for him to leave because he'll face a financial downfall, let him sit there in a sexless marriage with kids who don't respect him, paying taxes until he dies.

You have to remove the warrior spirit from men to control a

society. If these men had their warrior spirit they couldn't be controlled. They are going to say no.

This is the reality of it. I understand completely why, as a government, they've come along and encouraged social standards of one man with one woman, even though they know it's not biologically normal.

The human biological norm is that the top men have all the women, and the lower men have no women.

If you look at the history, if you actually look at the genes, something like 99% of females have reproduced since the dawn of human time, but only 23% of men.

So the point being that in the olden days, 23% of men had 99% of women. And that isn't necessarily a genetic thing. That's a power and success thing.

You can be a King. You don't have to be something special physically. You're the King, so you fuck all the girls. All those other dudes never got pussy. So the reason society comes along and says, one man-one woman, is for two reasons.

One is because it destroys the spirit of a man and avoids rebellion. And two, when you have a whole bunch of men who don't get laid, they're dangerous. They are the people who are going to revolt. They are the people who are gonna riot. The people who are gonna commit crime.

It's not good for a society as a whole if all these men can't get laid. For a long time we killed them off in wars and shit. But now everyone's living too long. So now men end up sat there miserable with their partner, too busy, too depressed, too sad, too self absorbed, too selfish to worry about the bigger picture.

·　·　·

THE REASON MEN haven't marched on the street because of Corona is because they're too busy, upset and sad because their woman's being mean to them. That's literally it.

It's also the reason they promote depression. Why do they promote mental illness at every corner? Because if you're so busy living inside your head, you don't give a fuck about what they do to you outside of your head. "I'm depressed, I'm sad. I'm anxious. I'm depressed, I'm sad. I'm anxious, poor me, me, me". So self-absorbed that they won't even think to rebel.

Why do the Western powers also promote diversity? If every single person who's inside a city, doesn't think the same, or look the same, or have any kind of common ideology, how can they rise up together? How can they all get together and band together against clear injustice?

They won't.

Diversity, feminism, matrimony. All this shit is deliberately designed to stop the men at the bottom realising they're getting fucked, and standing up and doing something about it.

That's all it is. It's completely a plan. It's been put together and the elites have pulled it off fantastically.

THE REASON FEMININITY is so promoted is because it's a direct competitor to masculinity. And the reason masculinity is directly attacked is very simple: Every single rebellion and revolution in history took place when men got pissed off and went to the streets. If you're the elites of the world, and there's only a few of you, and a lot of very pissed-off men, you have to make sure these men don't realise - "I'm working for fucking nothing, they've forced me to put a mask on, they've closed my business, they've taken my travel away".

If you want to do something like the coronavirus then you have to destroy masculinity absolutely. And you do that by taking one man, putting him with one woman, make it basically impossible for him to leave because he'll face a financial downfall, let him sit there in a sexless marriage with kids who don't respect him, paying taxes until he dies. You have to remove the warrior spirit from men to control a society. If these men had their warrior spirit they couldn't be controlled. They are going to say no.

This is the reality of it. I understand completely why, as a government, they've come along and said, look, one man, one woman, sit there even though they know it's not biologically normal. The human biological norm is that the top men have all the women and the lower men have no women. If you look at the history, if you actually look at the genes, something like 99% of females have reproduced since the dawn of human time, but only 23% of men.

SO THE POINT being that in the olden days, 23% of men had 99% of women. And that isn't necessarily a genetic thing. That's a power and success thing. You can be a King. You don't have to be something special physically. You're the King, so you fuck all the girls. All those other dudes never got pussy. So the reason society comes along and says, one man-one woman, is for two reasons. One is because it destroys the spirit of a man and avoids rebellion. And two, when you have a whole bunch of men who don't get laid, they're dangerous. They are the people who are going to revolt. They are the people who are gonna riot. The people who are gonna commit crime. It's not good for a society as a whole if all these men can't get laid. For a long time we killed them off in wars and shit. But now everyone's living too long. So now men end up sat there miserable with their partner, too busy, too depressed, too sad, too self absorbed, too selfish to worry about the bigger picture.

.   .   .

THE REASON MEN haven't marched on the street because of Corona is because they're too busy, upset and sad because their woman's being mean to them. That's literally it. It's also the reason they promote depression. Why do they promote mental illness at every corner? Because if you're so busy living inside your head, you don't give a fuck about what they do to you outside of your head. "I'm depressed, I'm sad. I'm anxious. I'm depressed, I'm sad. I'm anxious, poor me, me, me". So self-absorbed that they won't even think to rebel.

Why do the Western powers also promote diversity? If every single person who's inside a city, doesn't think the same, or look the same, or have any kind of common ideology, how can they rise up together? How can they all get together and band together against clear injustice?

They won't.

Diversity, feminism, matrimony. All this shit is deliberately designed to stop the men at the bottom realising they're getting fucked, and standing up and doing something about it.

That's all it is. It's completely a plan. It's been put together and the elites have pulled it off fantastically.

MY LIFE AS A PIMP

I've done a few things. I've lived a very eclectic life, Kickboxing champion, playboy, pimp. I'm happy with those labels so far, except the word pimp.

People always say pimp as if it's a negative thing. But I think a pimp is a very positive thing. I have to defend the reputation of pimps throughout history. I don't think they're bad people.

I just try and live as close as I can to my masculine imperative without hiding who I want to be, or what I want to do, or letting society program me. And I think if you give a man true free rein to completely be who he wants to be, and you don't let society program him, then he's gonna drive a fast car. He's gonna have a bunch of women, he's gonna do whatever we wants. We all want to be free. So I try my very best to be free.

AND ESPECIALLY IN the modern political climate with all this Corona, and shit.

I think freedom is being destroyed in real time. Even before Corona, freedom was being destroyed.

If you look at even very basic things. Like freedom of speech.

If a man isn't free to say what he thinks in the way he wants to say it, and express himself the way he wants, is he free? And what they do first is they restrict your speech. Because if they restrict your speech, then they can start to restrict your thoughts.

If you're not allowed to ever say it, then you're probably not going to think it so often. This is why it's done on purpose. So I don't think that society is very free at all. And I think that in regards to keeping our employment, keeping our money coming in, making sure we don't lose our social media accounts, every single person has to censor themselves to some degree.

And I try my very, very best to skirt that line, you know, as far as possible. So I feel free. Freedom is the ability to scream when you want to scream, be angry when you want to be angry, smile when you want to smile, say what you want, do what you want. And that's a very, very rare commodity in the modern world. That's extremely rare. So that's what I would consider free.

Early Days

So, I am half English, half American. My father was in the Air Force.

He was based at Chick Sands in the UK. He met my mother and they were fortunate enough to have this perfect child. I have a brother and a sister.

We moved back to America, and I lived the first ten years of my life in the United States. My father was a chess-master. That was his job. After he retired from the Air Force. He was a professional chess player.

So I GREW up around professional chess players, which is kind of an unusual climate to grow up in because you're growing up around all these ultra intelligent, semi autistic types. They're weirdos. You can't be that good at chess and be normal, right?

They're like human calculators. They're all a bit strange. And you have ex-KGB members and like, math nerds. And it's just a very weird kind of climate. So my father was a chess-master. But my father was very unique because my father was also a professional wrestler and had great physicality.

So you have, like, a bunch of dorks, then you have my Dad, who's this big black dude. And he's like, competing in the chess world.

So I grew up in a very kind of strange world. And I was a professional chess player also. Well I was on my path of being a professional chest player. At the age of five I was the state chess champion for Indiana, and I was the best ranked player under the age of ten. And I was on my way. So I played chess for the early part of my life.

And then at the age of eleven, my mother and father split up. My mom took me back to Luton. Great place. Lovely.

So from the age of eleven, I grew up in Luton, so that's the very beginning of the story.

A LOT of people talk about how stressful it was that their parents broke up.

I mean, I was very, very young. I don't think I was necessarily too upset by it. You know, my father was very honest and realistic with me. And he said, "OK, I'm still gonna see you but you're going to live in England". It is what it is.

So I don't think I was particularly upset by it. I definitely wouldn't say I was traumatised by it, but it did alter my life trajectory because I lost my chess coach. Up until then, I played chess 3, 4 hours a day.

All I did was chess, chess, chess. When we left, I found there was no chess scene in England like there is in America, where there's lots of chess in the school and these kind of things. There's no chess scene plus, I had no coach.

So for a while, I was kind of lost I would say. I had 4 hours free a day that I never used to previously have. And I mean, I didn't get into too much trouble or too much mischief, but I was certainly thinking how can I replace this thing I used to do all of the time? I ended up replacing it with fighting.

From around about 15, 16, I started kick boxing. And I think that fighting and chess are extremely similar. To me they aligned. They fulfilled the same gaps in my psyche.

People always ask how I went from being a chess player, which everyone sees as geeky, to being a kickboxer?

Well, chess is a one on one battle, right? That's all it is. There's no luck involved. There's no team, there's no wind that can blow the ball. It's one on one. It's a fight. If you lose, it's because you messed up.

And fighting feels the same for me. So I thought, Well, okay I can't learn chess well enough without a coach. And I can't find a coach in the UK who I trust to teach me chess. But I can find a coach who can teach me to kick people's ass. So that's kind of how it started.

Lots of people say they had aspirations of being the world champion at the beginning. I just turned up to training one step at a time. I just want to be good. So my coach said I had to train seven times a week.

So I just obeyed. I was just a worker ant. I just did as I was told. And then you win, and you win again, and you win again, and you get a title shot, you win.

And before you know it, you get up there. My first ever world title fight was on three days notice. Someone pulled out, and I had three days notice. I had to lose nine kilos in three days. Obviously, I was completely destroyed from the weight cut. Everyone expected me to lose, but I won. Then they gave the decision to the other guy. It was in France, and it was in Paris, and it was me against a French world champion.

They gave it to him, but I whooped his ass right. And we submitted the video to the ISKA, the organisation. And they demanded a rematch because it was so obvious I won. And we fought again. And without the big weight cut problem, I knocked him out in the 8th, and I became world champion for the first time.

It felt good. BuI I don't ever feel like I'm satisfied. I never won the world title and though "Yes, I'm the champ now". I was just like, okay, next. Next. Next.

I was kind of always like that. I always had these aspirations. I've always kind of felt there was something more. I'll explain....

Do you ever look around you and just look at the world and feel like we're in the Matrix, like there is something missing. Do you know what I mean?

Like everything just seems so superficial? And I don't know. I was always looking for this secret. I wouldn't say it was happiness or contentment, but I was always looking to try and break out of the nine to five, just the normal monotony of day to day life.

And for a long time, I thought fighting was my way out. I don't know what I was trying to get to. I don't know where it was gonna lead, but when I just look at the normal life that a lot of people live, that is just absolutely depressing to me.

I couldn't imagine doing it. I'm not shitting on the normal guy. I'm saying you're a stronger man than me, because of all the normal dude shit like working in Starbucks, bro, I couldn't do that. I couldn't do that day to day. I literally could not do that.

And I thought fighting will make sure I never have to do that. If that makes sense.

And there's always someone new to beat up. But then I'm dedicating all my time to fighting, which is actually the reason I retired.

I retired for four years. I came back last year and I fought three times, but I actually retired because one day I woke up and I looked at my life and I realised I'm giving 7 hours a day to fighting. If I were to put 7 hours a day into something else, what else could I achieve? Because I had a little bit of money from fighting, but I wasn't balling.

I wasn't RICH, rich. And I thought, What's the point being a world champion if I can't buy Lambos on the debit card? Right? What's the point?

So then I thought, I want to be rich now. So that's actually the reason I retired. I was always chasing other things. And now I've got money, I want to fight again. I'm never happy. This is how it goes. You're always chasing something else. But I do feel like to a degree, I have at least partially escaped the Matrix I used to talk about.

I kind of feel like I've started to escape. And Corona, as much as it's been a headache for everybody, has helped me realise how fortunate I am in my position when everyone else is locked down. I can just get on a private jet and go where I want. So that it is kind of cool when they go, "There's no flights". I'm like, "Maybe not for you!. There are flights for me". So I feel like I've semi-escaped, so I've kind of got there.

∾

Think About Money

So, let's talk about the webcam business.

I was 28 when I won my fourth world title. And one day I woke up and I looked at my bank account. I mean, I just won a world title fight, but I hadn't fought in six months.

I had like, three grand, four grand in there. And it felt like I was giving up my entire life. I don't even know how I'm going to live. I need to get rich. I want to get rich.

So I told my coach I was going to take a couple of months off, and I'm going to focus purely on money. I'm sitting with my brother. And I'm like, how can we get rich?

NOW THAT I HAVE MONEY, lots of people always ask me, how do I get rich? And I ask, When's the last time you talked about money, When's the last time you sat down with your friends and refuse to talk about anything else but how to make money? How are you making money? How is he making money? How am I making money? How can we make money together? How's that guy making money? How's that coffee shop there making money?

Do they sell cake? No. Why don't they sell cake? Everyone in here is a businessman. If they had a cute young waitress, a girl instead of a guy, they'd probably sell more coffee.

No one analyses anything. They just want to get rich, right? They want to be rich, but they have no plan to get rich. And a hope and a plan are very different things. I explain this to people all the time. Everyone has a dream, but no one has a plan. And nothing good is gonna happen on accident, right?

I didn't become world champion on accident. I didn't wake up and there I was, a champion. You have to plan for it.

So I said to Tristan, we need to discuss money. We need to

plan this, and we need to work out a way we can get rich. And that's when I started analysing and understanding banks and the credit system and the money system, how the world actually works. And then I got really pissed off because I realised that money isn't real and it's all a scam.

The banks are destroying us in real time with inflation. And I still don't have any.

So I was really mad. I was writing things down as I was watching some YouTube videos, like financial advice. And we're talking about assets, liabilities, etc.

And I'm writing down all my assets, and I'm trying to work out what I have that's worth money. And the only thing I wrote down was my car. But what's that worth? Nothing.

I'm big and strong, but I'm already fighting. I can't think of anything else to do with that.

THE ONLY THING I HAD, due to fighting all around the world, were these six girlfriends.

Because you'd win the world title, then you'd fuck a ring girl. She falls in love with you and thinks that you're the big millionaire in London. Thinks you're living the balling life. When really you're in some tiny, tiny apartment with a door lock.

So I had these girlfriends, and I thought, Well, I can't open a strip club, it costs money to open a strip club. And I'm kind of racking my brain.

And by absolute coincidence, I'm going around the Internet, and I saw in the corner this "Talk to live girls now" advert.

I was never a porn guy. I've never been watching porn or clicking on these things. So I clicked on it. And there's some chick there on a computer like," Hi!" And I was like, "My girls can do that". So that was the very beginning. That was the

Eureka moment. When Tristan came home I said, "We're going to start a webcam company".

AND THIS IS the thing that's interesting about it, because when people hear this story and they call me a pimp, etc, they imagine me to be this exploitative, horrible, evil man, which is absolutely and utterly the complete opposite.

I'm not trying to convince anyone I'm a nice guy, because I don't give a shit. I'm just telling the truth.

So the beginning of it was I messaged my six girlfriends and told them they're all coming to live with me. And I had a job for them in London.

Two of them wouldn't come. Four of them agreed. I told them "We're gonna make a bunch of money, you're gonna live with me. Blah, blah, blah". So I'm in this shitty apartment, you know, cause kickboxing's, not boxing. You're not making millions like the boxers are.

So the four girls flew in. I sat them all down at a table. They're all like, "Who's this chick? Who's this chick?" Told them all the truth. I just straight sat there , just sat there and said, "Listen, I've been with you all. I'm starting a webcam business. I'm gonna get rich. Some of you are gonna come with me to the top of the mountain, or if you're pissed off you can fucking fly home". It was very matter-of-fact. At this point I hadn't agreed to take another fight, so I need money now.

Anyway, two of them left, two of them agreed to stay. And the beginning of my Cam Empire was this tiny little apartment with me and my two girlfriends.

SO THEY WENT on Cam together as a duo, as a team to start making money. And that was the beginning of it.

The interesting thing about it was these girls were so inept from a business perspective. They were very beautiful, and they're nice girls and I can't say anything bad about them. But women do not have a business mind.

So they'd sit on Webcam, and an old dude would watch them. And the old dude would say, "What kind of guy do you like?"

And they'd say, "Oh, I don't know, someone in shape who's rich and young". And I'd be like, no, no, he's an old dude. You have to say, "I'm tired of these young guys messing me around. I need an older guy who's ready to settle down. I don't care if he has money as long as he'll take care of me".

Conversely, If he's a young guy, you say "I'm tired of these old guys perving on me". You need to sell the dream. So I'm training these girls, and it got to the point where it was easier if I just typed myself.

So what we ended up doing was we had the two girls on camera with a keyboard, which wasn't plugged in.

And then I was behind the screen talking to the dudes saying the right things and dragging money out the Internet. It was like mind blowing to me. And I'm sitting there typing, and I've typed 16, 17 hours a day. But I pulled in, let's say, three grand a day, four grand a day.

So that became my new life, right? I went from kickboxer to fucking pretending to be a girl on the internet for about three months. I'm just typing, typing until the girls learn. And once the girls learn, they could do it themselves. Then I thought, now I need some more chicks.

And that was the beginning of the Cam Empire.

～

Growth Of The Empire

So the most girls I had at any one point, was 75.

I had four premises, and I had 75 girls on the books. They weren't all working at once. But I had 75 girls who would do, like, one shift a week, or three days a week, or seven days a week.

75 women working for me at the peak of it all.

But that was a mistake, because when you have a bunch of girls working for you like that, the only way you can motivate them is with money. And it was better when I started, because the girls worked for me because they loved me.

That's the old school pimp game, isn't it? They think "I love this man. We're on our way to the top together. We're gonna go to the Maldives,we're making all this money". You know, it's the old school dream. But when you get too big, you can't have all these girls in love with you.

So then you have to motivate them with money. And if you're trying to motivate a woman with money, it's impossible.

And any feminists will disagree with me. But I'll tell you something, women are loyal to one thing on the planet. The only thing they're loyal to is the man they want to have sex with, that is it.

If a woman's working for you and she's making ten grand a week, but the man who's banging her is like, "I don't want you doing all that. Who's the fuck is this guy that's pimping you out?"

They're gonna quit.

Or he'll say, "We can do it together", even though they can't. Because there's a whole bunch of people think it's easy, right? It's not easy. You need equipment.

You need to sort out the tax, the banking. You need to know how to handle the customers. It's not easy to do. Every time there was a girl who I wasn't sleeping with, she never lasted long.

So now I had these four big premises, all these overheads, all these managers that got out of control.

Eventually I had to cut it down to a special-forces team of around eight girls. And that's where I made my most money. When I had four girlfriends, and my brother had four girlfriends. Me and my brother, with eight women living in one house. And all the women adored us. And they obeyed us. And at the peak, I was turning over 400 grand a month with eight girls.

And people always ask if those girls slept with any other people, seeing as me and Tristan were sleeping with four each.

No, they didn't. That's cheating. A woman can't do that. That's cheating. I can do it because i'm a man. If a woman sleeps with multiple people, that's cheating. That's absolutely unacceptable on every level. That's unacceptable.

MEN AND WOMEN are not the same. We've never been the same. This new idea that men and women are the same is complete garbage.

For the longest period of human history, men had a role and women had a role. Men have never been faithful. Ever. Look at history. Every single King, every single Sultan had more than one woman.

Look at the history, read the Bible. All there. Never in any point in history was a woman with several men and it be deemed acceptable. Female promiscuity has always been frowned upon since the dawn of human time.

In fact, only a hundred years ago, you couldn't get married unless you were a virgin. It was the only thing that mattered because it ensures paternity. Before paternity tests. how else do you know that the kid is yours unless she was a virgin? It's the only way to be sure.

For the longest period of human time, the idea of a promiscuous female has been frowned upon and shamed. In half of the world today it's still shamed. So a woman can't go around fucking people and pretend it's the same as a man running around fucking people.

It is absolutely not the same.

A man can only cheat if he loves someone else. If I have a woman who I truly love, and I go out and fuck someone I don't care about and then come back to her, that's not cheating. That's exercise.

But if she even talks to a dude then it is cheating. Because females are emotionally invested. I have no emotional investment. So, no, and I'll make this very, very clear: Any woman who was with me never spoke to any man besides me and my brother, and the men that were paying them online.

That is it. They were absolutely loyal to me. And if they weren't, they got fired.

So how does a man get this to happen? You get that to happen through showing competence. Every single thing in life is a value exchange, every single thing. Even friendships. You both gain something through your interaction, right? Either it makes you feel happy, or he can help you with some things, or you help each other. Every single thing in life's a value exchange. So I have to provide value for these women for them to want to be with me. You can't just be some jackass.

People have this idea that, oh, you're a pimp. You just get these girls, you put them to work and they're scared of you.

It's bullshit. I was doing this in London. A girl could've walked out the door any day, or called the police on me any day, but they didn't. They wanted to be with me because they genuinely understood that their life was better if they obeyed me.

They genuinely trusted me. And they genuinely also understood that if they're gonna be with any kind of high-value man that he's gonna fucking cheat anyway. So why hide it? Isn't it easier to know the bitch? Isn't it easier to at least suck her tits a bit and join in? Like, what's the point in fooling yourself and pretending your man's loyal when he's out doing whatever anyway, there's no difference.

So I know it seems extreme, but these girls are making good money. They're living a very good life. They were with a man they loved along with these other girls who were their best friends.

And it was a pretty happy environment overall. Although when you're the patriarch of that kind of environment, you do have to do a lot of policing. But all in all, there was no disrespect in the house. There was no arguments in the house. I wouldn't tolerate a negative environment. That's bad for business.

There's not gonna be any Debbie Downer around, pissing everyone off because they're not gonna smile on camera. So it was a very happy interaction. And my girls just understood "Look, I'm fucking you all. If you don't like it, leave".

AND TO ADDRESS another constant question- When I had the 75 cam girls working for me, did I sleep with them all?

No, I couldn't. There's too many. There's no way. It was impossible.

I was probably only sleeping with five or six. I tried to go like, very legit businessman with them and not sleep with them all.

But that's when I learned my lessons, right? I learned so many lessons from that period of my life about male and female dynamics. So many lessons. And I learned women are loyal to the dick they wanna suck and nothing else, and if they're not having sex with you, they're gonna have sex with somebody else.

They're not gonna go sexless. And whoever they're having sex with is the person they're gonna listen to ultimately. And that person does not want them naked in another dude's house. Why would they?

So I was trying to motivate girls with money. The girls who loved me and worked for me, my main girlfriends, they get probably around 20% of their money. I'd keep 80% of the money they made. So they basically work for free. They worked for my love and attention. The other girls were the other way around.

I'D KEEP 20% for all the help I gave them, the premises, the typing, because by that time I had a room of typists. I had like, four or five girls who were full time professional typists. They were ugly, but they were smart. And then I had the pretty girls on the cameras.

So I had, like, a professional setup. I was taking 20% of the money from them and they got 80%. So I was trying to motivate them with money. But motivating with money doesn't work for two reasons.

The first reason is, if a girl has no romantic interest in you, the idea of you making money off of her tits, offends her. Like you're using her tits. It's like grabbing a girl's tits who doesn't like you. Do you understand what I mean? There's something weird about it. They didn't like it.

I'd buy a new car and they'd be like, this fucking guy, why is he getting a car? Even though I was getting a minuscule cut for the amount of work I did for them. I was getting very small amounts from these girls because these are the girls who I didn't have romantic interest in.

That was the first thing. So they were abrasive. They're idiots.

And the second thing is, the man they're sleeping with is always like, "Hey, why the fuck are you working for this guy? We can do this ourselves. You can do this yourself. He's exploiting you".

Because they don't want the fucking girl working for me. And what's amazing is every single time a girl quit you'd see them fail.

They would be working for me, making ten grand a month, and they'd be keeping eight grand. I took two grand.

Then they'd quit and try to do it with their boyfriend, make one grand a month, and then quit again. Every single one who stopped working for me ended up failing and begging for her job back. 100%.

So I started having firing-girls parties. I understood the psychology of women, and women as a whole are absolutely group thinkers.

Females are sheep. Everyone says women are complicated. No they are not. Women are programmable. Women are blank slates, and they're either programmed by you as a man, or they're programmed by society. The good wife who obeys her man and cooks for him and cleans for him has been programmed by her man.

The woman who goes, "I don't need no man, I'm a feminist" has been programmed by society and by the BBC. They're programmed, they're all born blank. And someone inserts the programming.

. . .

So with my women, because of the group think, every single time a girl would get fired or quit, we'd have a party.

And when you have a party about the girl quitting, all the girls would stand around and laugh. "Oh, she's going to end up asking for her job back. She doesn't appreciate what Andrew did for her. Ha ha ha".

So then girls didn't want to quit because they knew there'd be a party about them, and they didn't want that. I had girls come to me saying, "Look, I have to leave. I'm sorry. I really have to leave, please don't throw a party". They were so scared of all the girls who used to know them, mocking them behind their back.

I never exploited anybody. I never hit a girl. I never hurt anybody. I didn't even have to raise my voice.

I was a positively inspirational and motivating person. I was a P.I.M.P.. I made them feel happy doing what they did. They liked working for me. So that was it. It was a very happy environment. There was no slavery element.

You're not going to get a girl to work 12 hours a day, six days a week by being mean to her.

It's not like porn. I think if a girl turns to porn, then she's had a hard life. Why would you want to be railed left, right, and centre by fuck knows who on camera?

I think there's something wrong with that. I don't think that's a natural feminine mindset. I don't think any woman who's normal in her brain wants that.

But with the webcam side, I genuinely had girls who worked for me, who previously had a long-term boyfriend, or had only slept with two men in their lives.

It's not like people imagine it to be. 99% of being a Cam girl is much more like a therapist than a porn star. Yes, she can make money from showing her tits, whatever. But she makes the big money from making these guys *like* her. By being funny, playful banter, being good friends, messing around.

I had girls who would paint pictures and sell the painting. I had girls who played piano. It was not as sexual as people think it was.

It was very much like guys falling in love with them on the internet.

And it wasn't even about private chats. If you're a good girl, and you're very good at the job, you'd get loyal fans who really loved you. They'd be there every single day. And they wouldn't even be buying your time. They'd just be donating money.

Plus, it's safe. There's rules on these websites. Men can't ask for bestiality. They can't ask for kiddy shit. They can't ask for anything too weird.

ONE OF MY best girls had a guy called Paul. I think he was from Scotland. And here's what Paul got up to..

So, Paul sent her $500. Just tipped it to her bank. $500, "Please can you buy some gummy bears?"

So she bought some gummy bears. And the next day he said, "Okay, here's what I want you to do". And he took her private, for $5 a minute.

So I think all in all, he was on there for another $500 worth. This was a $1000 interaction.

He got the girl to line up all the gummy bears and pretend that they were him and all his friends.

So she's sitting here with her tits out, and all the gummy bears lined up.

And she'd have to pick up one of the friends. And she's saying "He looks tasty!" And then Paul is like, "Please don't eat my friend. Please don't eat my friend!". And she'd reply, "But he looks good".

"Please, please, please don't". And you'd see him on camera. He's like, jerking off.

"Please, please, please don't". And she's putting it on her lips and between her tits, then licking it. Poor Paul is literally about to come everywhere from this.

Eventually she starts chewing his friend, eating his friend, and he loved it. "Please don't, please stop eating me. Please stop eating me!", until finally she's eaten all the friends.

Finally it's down to Paul. He's the last guy. And he begs, "Please don't eat me. Please. I'll do anything. Please. I'll give you more money. Please don't eat me!"

She's like, "No, I'm gonna eat you". And after about two minutes of threatening she eats Paul, and he comes all over the place.

So, I mean, you get that kind of thing.

It's a bit weird, but it's funny. Like, who gives a shit, right? The girl thinks it's funny. No one took it that seriously. The idea that these women on webcam are like, sexually abused or forced to do it is wrong.

I literally had a girl who was a waitress at Nando's who just wanted more money.

She came and did it, and thought it was funny to talk to Paul and listen to his bullshit. Then a bunch of men in America fell in love with her and they didn't even know her real name.

She made a lot of money. It can be that cool. I'm telling you, I can assure you, because I lived it.

MOST GIRLS just came from me and my brother living our lives. We lived a very good life. We attracted female attention.

And every time we dated a girl, we just say, look, do you want do this? If they said no, then okay, cool. If they said yes. We'd say, okay, cool. That was it. We were the head recruiters.

. . .

So HOW I can believe in love, having all these girls?

I completely believe in love. I'm a massive advocate for love. I'm a massive advocate for men and women being in love with each other. I'm not one of those evil predators, or a playboy who thinks women are just for sex. Not at all.

If you get ill, if you're sick in bed, the first thing you do is call a woman, right?

You don't call your boys. Like, there's a very sacred interaction between men and women.

I love the idea of family. I love the idea of children. I love the idea of being in love with a woman. I love the idea of her loving me. I just don't see why I should only love only one. I don't see why I can't love five.

I'm just very honest. I don't think I'm any worse than most other men. I just think I tell the truth. I just think I've realised that cheating and hiding is too much fucking work.

Just to say, "Look, my dear, I love you with all my heart. We're gonna be together forever. And yeah I fucked that bitch. I don't even know her name." Whatever.

I mean, they can either go crazy and leave, or they don't go crazy and stay. It's a binary decision.

When I say this, people really don't believe it. "Oh but that means the girl doesn't really love you". That's not true. If she didn't really love me, she'd leave. She completely loves me. What women are looking for is wanting to feel special.

Sexual exclusivity is how a woman proves to a man that he is special to her.

"You are my man. So I only sleep with you". But what we've now done in the modern world is say "You also need to prove she's special so you have to only sleep with her".

But if she knows she's special in other ways, then she doesn't give a fuck what you do. And this is really not revolutionary.

You might think that my girls don't really love me. That's not true. I know my women love me. I know they've been loyal to me.

I've had two girls who started with me at the beginning. Eight years. I'm still with them to this day. If you go to Russia, for example, and see high-value men, do you think these mafia guys in Russia are loyal? Do you think Putin's loyal, these big boys? No, it's accepted over there. You speak to a Russian girl, she's like, "Oh, he's rich. Of course he has his fun but I am his wife".

It's normal. Completely normal. It's only in countries like America and England where a woman's gonna go, "I would never take that. I'd never accept that".

Oh, you're gonna let a man pay for your entire life? You're gonna drive his Mercedes? You're gonna have this fucking big G, but if he talks to some bitch one night while he's out drunk, you're gonna fucking pretend that that's the worst thing in the world?

That's Western bullshit feminist thinking. The feminism element doesn't exist in most places in the world. If you go to Russia every single high level guy has fucking three or four mistresses, all of them.

It doesn't have to hurt people's feelings. I don't think it does. I can tell you now, honestly and utterly.

Let's say I have a girl, and I take her on holiday. I look after her. She's financially looked after. She's the only girl I sleep next to. I don't sleep next to or hug other women, I just fuck them sometimes. And she genuinely, genuinely doesn't care anymore. She's like, okay, whatever.

Everyone knows she's the Queen. She's with me all over Instagram. Everyone knows she's my main girl, and she really genuinely doesn't care. There's no unhappiness. I know people believe that's an impossible scenario to set up, but it really isn't.

Because what's funny is this: Girls always say, "I'd never take that crap. I'd never put up with that".

I say, all right, go to your man right now and demand to see his phone. I bet he's gonna make excuses. Say we're gonna swap phones for a week. He's just say, "Oh, no because of work. No, no, no".

Don't buy that shit. He's making excuses, he doesn't want you to see something. And you know what that is? That's pussy. You know it. And I know it.

So go in there and demand it.

"Well, yeah, I trust him". No, you don't trust him. You just don't want to see the truth, because you already know what he's doing.

Every woman who's with a fucking G already knows what he's doing, they just lie to themselves and pretend to be blind.

The difference between me and them is that my girl hasn't got to live in a fucking fantasy.

She knows. Those women who pretend to not know are no better than my woman who actually knows.

In fact, I'd say my woman who actually knows is smarter than those bimbos who sit there and pretend.

The Man's Role

Which brings us onto equality.

I don't think the world has ever been equal. I do believe we should have equal rights under the law. I'm not saying that women should be slaves. I'm saying that the modern society we live in has been built by men.

Let's cut the crap. All the roads you see, all the buildings, everything around you. Men built all of it. Then women come along and say, oh we were just as important.

You are just as important. But you do a completely different role. You fulfilled a different role in society.

And I think now, if you look at the roles of society, I believe men are still doing their job, but I don't know if women are doing their job.

A woman's job was always procreation and to look after the family, to look after the men. That's all that they had to do.

And the man would go out there and risk his life and spend his time building the modern world.

Men are still out here building the modern world. But when they come home now, the girls are like, "Oh, why should I cook for you?"

I think women are failing in their role. And thats down to the propaganda that's being propagated by the system. The Western world is convincing women that they're a high-value woman if they don't take shit from a man, don't look after a man, and work really hard in their career.

And I just think that's asinine. Why wouldn't you want to work really hard for your babies and for your man, as opposed to working in some business which doesn't even care about you?

I THINK a man's role on this planet is also another thing that we need to redefine to some degree.

A man's role has changed. But from the dawn of human time, a man's role has always been the capability for violence. This is what men were, right. When I look at the world, I look at it from a societal perspective, and I look at it from an animalistic perspective. Society has told us to be certain ways. And then our animal instinct tells us to be another way.

. . .

So society tells you to marry one woman and be loyal. And then you have me saying men are not supposed to do that. They don't want to do that. Any man who sits there and says he wants to do that is lying.

He wants to keep the woman he loves, and he wants the woman he loves to be happy, of course. But if he could keep the woman he loves, and keep her happy, and have other women, he would.

You're lying if you say that's not true.

So from an animal perspective, a man's primary role was the capability for violence. We went to war, we conquered stuff. We built stuff. That's what men did. We conquered.

To this day still, if you look at men, many of them are still trying to conquer the world one way or another.

Why does the CEO work 15 hours a day for some fucking conglomerate? Well, the women don't want to work that much. Or they'll work hard, but they want to also have a life outside of work.

Why do men give up their lives for work? Is it just for money or is it because they feel important and they feel like they're conquering? This is what I'm saying. Men have that drive inside of them. And this is since the dawn of human time.

Why did I fight? Why do men climb Mt. Everest? Why did the Romans melt rocks, make swords and walk in random directions to find somebody, anybody, to fuck them up and take their stuff.

This is who we are.

So this is what men always were. And I think now that's been redefined. Obviously, we want to live in a peaceful society now, right? We can't just run around with swords.

So a lot of the male instinct to conquer Earth is financial. I think this is why men work so hard, this is why men are so obsessed with money. Or they should be. They absolutely should be obsessed with money.

AND IF YOU'RE a guy who's working a 9 to 5, married with kids, and going on holiday twice a year, and you're truly happy, then congratulations. I would genuinely say congratulations if you're happy with that.

I know that's like a pretty normal setup, and I don't look down on you. That's perfectly fine. But some men are just not born that way. Some men are born with something else inside of them. A fire inside of them, which cannot be extinguished by beans on toast ,TV at night, nine to five, sitting around with your wife, a couple of blow jobs a month. Some men are not satisfied with that.

Myself as an individual, I could not be satisfied with that. That doesn't mean I look down on the people who are. Absolutely congratulations.

But my time on the planet, I guarantee, will be more eventful. I will die with more stories. I will have made a bigger ripple in space and time, because I refuse to comply with just the average. There's always been that average class of person since the dawn of time. There's always been the normal guy.

And then there's been the dude who insists on conquering the world. There's been Napoleon who says "No, fuck you. I'm taking this and this and this". It depends what you're born with.

YOU MAY ASK "Where does it end?" Making over half a million a month, sleeping with girls everywhere. Lamborghinis, Ferraris, houses all around the world.

Why does it need to end? I think a man should have absolutely no interest in whether he's actually happy or not. If I wake up and I'm unhappy, I will do the exact same things as if I am happy.

I will go to the gym, I will work.

How I feel has no impact on how I live my life. I don't think happiness as an index is a healthy view for a man to have on life success.

Women are different. Women just want to be happy. Women just want to smile. They don't care how. They don't care if they deserve it or not, as long as they get to smile.

But I think for a man, if you're waking up and asking if you're happy, then you're looking at life wrong.

For a man, if you move happiness down the scale and you start looking at, am I successful? Am I competent? Am I achieving things? Am I respected?

If you start to look at these indicators of your life instead, you're gonna end up being happier without actually analysing if you're happy or not.

So for me, I understood very very well that half a million dollars a month is good, but a million dollars a month is better.

And I also very much understood that as soon as you stop pushing forward, as soon as you go stagnant, you're dying. As soon as you stay in one place, you're slowly on the way down.

You have to grow at all times. So every business has to work. As I became successful I was under enormous pressure.

I didn't think, oh, I have plenty of money now. It was the complete opposite. I want to work harder. More hours. I found the tap.

If there was a golden tap, with unlimited money, and you had a bucket, would you just fill that one bucket? Or would you run back, get another bucket, and so on?

I couldn't stop. I couldn't sleep. I would wake up to piss at three in the morning, and by time I finished pissing, after only three hours sleep, I'd wake up the girls and put them back online.

I couldn't get it out of my brain because I saw that I had replaced fighting, which I loved, with this. And this was my chance to escape the Matrix. This has been inside of me since as early as I can remember.

SO NOW WHEN I drive my Ferrari, I'm like, this is the full circle. This is the universe giving me what I've always been manifesting. Does that make sense?

I have every brand of supercar you can fucking name. I have 17 cars. I have over $10 million of cars. But when I didn't have them, these cars used to piss me off. So now I have to have them all.

I don't need to drive them. But I have to have them. I'm trying to conquer the Earth. Maybe I'm crazy, but this is what I'm trying to do and what I've always been trying to do.

So I've never been satisfied. To this day I'm making more money now than I was making in the cam days.

SO I DON'T JUDGE my life on happiness. I don't look at it that way.

I look at all the other human metrics and say, Where am I failing? Am I in good shape? Yeah. Am I rich? Yeah. Do I have good friends? Good connections? Yeah. Do I do whatever I want? Am I free? Tick, tick, tick, tick, tick, tick, tick. Well, fuck it, then. Life is fine.

I will pass any lie detector test today that I'm the most content happy man in the world. Cause that's what I've decided. That's what I've labeled myself as. So how can it not be true?

. . .

THERE'S ONLY one thing on the planet you actually have control over.

You can't control the weather. You can't control your health. You can get a brain aneurysm or a heart attack. You can't control other people.

The only thing you can actually really, truly control is what you think. That's the only thing you can change in real time. You can be thinking of red and change it to blue.

So why are you not controlling your own mind? It's your asset. It's your ally. It's your friend. Why would you make an enemy out of the only thing you have control over?

I refuse to do that. It doesn't make sense to me. The worst thing on Earth that could happen to a man could happen to me. And I guarantee you I would still label myself happy.

I'm happy because that's who I am. That's how I view myself. That's what I've decided.

~

Bucharest

So, I'm disenfranchised with the west.

I'm anti-West. My political views are completely anti-Western. I think that the West is on a serious moral and economic decline, and I would rather live in a society which I see is on the way up rather than on the way down.

I think America is becoming more and more violent by the day. Taxes are getting higher and higher, police powers and police control are getting more and more strict.

We're living in a society where you have to be scared of the criminals, scared of the police, scared of the tax man. Scared of everything. And I don't see what the benefit of living there is. I don't see it. Same in England.

You look at London ten years ago, compared to London now.

I can't wear a nice watch in London. Not like I used to be able to, it's not safe at night. Most places now I'm risking getting stabbed to pay 60% taxes.

And then on top of that, the police want to give me a fine for not wearing a mask. It's a police state. If I'm going to live in a police state, I want at least to be provided with safety.

If I go to Dubai, it's a police state, but it's safe. I can wear a million dollar watch all day long.

I know I can't fuck with the law, but at least they've given me my safety.

In the West, they're gonna take all your freedom and not provide safety, and then they want to police your Facebook comments. Why would I stay there? I have money. I don't need to stay there.

So as soon as I realised I didn't need to stay there, I started looking at the world. And you realise the world is small. Because all the problems I just described in Western Europe, America, and Canada are all the same.

In South America if you're flexing and living a good life, you're risking getting your head chopped off.

Australia is a fucking penal colony. Fuck them. South-East Asia? A lot of it's crap. I mean, I don't wanna bang Thai girls and run around in the sand.

So you start running out of places. And then you start looking, and the only places to really live that I've enjoyed in my life are Dubai, but that's just one city so you can get bored, or Russia and Eastern Europe.

In Eastern Europe it's very much a safe place unless you piss off the wrong boys.

In England, crime can be very random. You can be walking down the street. Wrong place, wrong time, you get stabbed. In Romania, the chance of a random attack is zero.

But if you fuck with the wrong guy, you're gonna disappear. But that's the same everywhere in the world, right? If you fuck with the wrong guy.

So I would rather live in a society knowing that I have to respect certain people, but the chance of random violence is zero. Rather than England, where you're still have to respect certain people, but there's a random violence element.

So I knew some very important guys in Romania. You can't just rock up to Ukraine, start pushing a Lambo, start fucking a bunch of girls and not have trouble.

But in Romania, I had good friends to make sure that it didn't happen. I had very good friends there from fighting, and we became business partners on a bunch of other things.

And now it is what it is. So I feel very, very safe there. 100%.

AND FOR THE most beautiful girls I would say either Russia or Moldova.

But I would clarify that if you're reading this and you want to go to visit, they're very difficult to sleep with. They're not stupid.

I'm telling you, people really have this view of Eastern European girls as sluts, because a lot of them are working girls.

Yeah, maybe if you go to Dubai, or if you go to a brothel in Germany, and there's a bunch of Romanian girls.

Let me tell you, Romanian girls are not sluts. They're smart. If a Romanian girl wants to be a slut she does it for money. And if she doesn't do it for money and she's not a slut, she's exceptionally hard to sleep with.

A lot of these girls in Bucharest are around 25 or 26. They've got two or three men body counts. They don't sleep around. They're very hard to get.

If they want to be a hoe, they're gonna be a hoe and get

paid. Only an English or an American girl is stupid enough to be a hoe for free.

A Western girl will be a hoe cause they were drunk. They'll just be a hoe cause they're dumb. In Eastern Europe they're far too intelligent for that. They understand that the number one commodity a female has is beauty. And if they're born with it, they're not gonna fucking waste it going out getting hammered and banging Joe Whoever.

They're not gonna do that, they're not stupid like that.

So Western girls are extremely easy to sleep with compared to Eastern European women. Eastern European women are much, much harder. They're more savvy. And people say that they're gold diggers. But that's not true.

I would say that if a woman from Romania, or Ukraine, or Russia is gonna be dating you, she is genuinely considering if there's a future for marriage and babies, because they still have that element of society where women are respected as a mother. They want to be mothers.

So if you have no money, why would they want a family with you? They want someone who can financially provide for them to have a family from him. Can this man pay for me?

So, yeah, they do respect money, but they're much harder to sleep with. So don't think you're gonna go over there and find a girl to sleep with on the first night.

It's gonna be hard, very difficult. You have to date them for a long time. They want to go on lots of dates. They want to really know you. It's harder over there.

And Moldova I wouldn't go to cause Moldova is probably the most hostile place I've ever been. I've been there three times and I was attacked twice.

They are super right-wing nationalist. And you know what's crazy? Even though they attacked me, I respect them for it.

. . .

So me and my brother were in Moldova and it was two in the morning. We had these three girls with us. We're walking and talking to the girls in English, and this guy comes by and goes, "Oh, American."

And I say, "Hi". He shouts, "Oh, you come here to bang bang. You come here porno. Yeah. You come here porno". And by the time he said that, four of his friends got out of a car and they jumped us.

Because they knew - Americans have come to this shit-hole country to fuck our women. Why else would I be there? They know exactly why I was there and I knew why I was there. Everyone understood the interaction.

And the Moldovan men have the attitude of, Fuck you! We're not gonna let you come here and just bang our women.

Why would they? They're super, super nationalistic, Super, super right wing.

And that's happened to me twice. They came at us. They punched me. I took it. Then they punched my brother. We got them all on one side so we weren't surrounded and then we're like, "Okay, we're leaving. Sorry. We're leaving."

My brother speaks Romanian. They spoke Romanian and Russian. My brother said, "We're not tourist, we're not tourists" in Romanian.

That threw them off a little bit. And we got in the taxi. The girls also got in the taxi and came with us.

So we got the taxi. Tristan's lip's bleeding a little bit. Nothing too big. We got back to the hotel, and one of the girls started telling the hotel receptionist what happened. And then what was scary is the hotel receptionist started to panic.

She's asked, "What car were they in?" I replied, "a BMW".

She was like "Oh no!". Because over there the average wage is like $200 month. Having a BMW is a big deal.

"Oh a BMW. They might be Mafia guys. They're going to come here. They're gonna come after you. They're going to come after you".

And we're asking, "How are they going to know that we're here?", and the receptionist says, "The taxi now is going to go back to them and say, for a tip, they'll tell them you're here".

Then she started really having a panic attack. So we say to call the police, but she goes, no, no, she didn't want to call the police. So now me and Tristan are scared because the receptionist is freaking out.

It was 4am on a Saturday morning, and there was a flight back to Romania at 06:00 a.m. So we just packed and bailed. It was a case of "all right, shit. Let's get out of here!".

And twice similar stories have happened to me in Moldova. Moldovans are super protective of their people and their culture.

And so when I walk through London and look at all the problems we have there, I have to respect those guys. Because they won't let anyone go there and fuck around with them, or disrespect them, or fuck their women or anything.

And the girls, they are ten out of ten. They're fucking beautiful. But they're kind of trapped there. They can't get out and the men won't let us in.

But I respect them. I really respect them as men. If I ever meet those guys who jumped me, I'll shake his hand, I get it. I get it.

～

Casinos

In Romania, I have 15 branches of a casino. There's no live dealers. It's just machines. So it's like an arcade set up. Corona came and fucked that up. So I've been paying 15 rents for a year and a half.

I wanted to open that business for a long time. And it's weird how it started. This actually feeds back into what we were saying earlier about analysing money.

So I own 10% of RXF, which is the Romanian UFC. I own a percentage of a cage-fighting organisation.

I do the the English commentary for the fights. And one of the main sponsors of the events is this casino brand. This casino brand is owned by three brothers, and they have 400 locations from Estonia all the way down the east of Europe. I overheard them say they turn over 18 million a day or something.

Ridiculous money.

So I spoke to them, because they're sponsoring the show. "Ok, guys, I want to open some casinos. I want to get involved in this money maker".

And they kind of looked at me. Typical Eastern European Mafia. Fat, bald, with a cigar. Exactly like you'd imagine them to be.

And they're like, "Why do we need you? If I want to open a location, I send a picture to a WhatsApp group of a building, and two weeks later, there's a location. What do I need you for?"

I thought, okay, valid point. Well, I'm going to find a reason for them to need me, right? So a few years go past, we're kind of talking back and forth.

They won't let me franchise with them. They're not interested. And then I came up with this plan. I went to them one day and I said, "Look, how about this? I'll pay to open a location, so it costs you no money to be involved. I'll give you a percentage of turnover, not just profits, so even if it makes no money, you're making money because it's pure turnover. And I'll open up directly next door to your number one competitor in Romania. So I'm gonna go to war for you with my money because I'm right next door to your competitor. The location may not make money. I'll lose all my money, but you're getting a percent of turnover. You ain't got to do anything. It doesn't cost you anything. You make money, and it's just pissing your competitor off. Worst case is that I annoy number two in the country, right?"

And they agreed. So I opened up next door to the competitor, and then I have to try and make money. So now this goes back into what I was saying earlier, because people always say to me, "How do you make money Tate?" You have to sit and genuinely think and analyse.

So I OPEN up this casino next door to my competitor. And two doors down there's a Starbucks.

The queue for Starbucks is going out the door. Starbucks is always busy. Okay. So I put a huge sign up, a massive sign saying "free coffee".

I had a really cute little waitress, and I bought a very expensive coffee machine.

So what happened is because the line for Starbucks was so long, the dudes would go "Oh I'll just get free coffee in here". And then they gambled their money instead of buying the coffee.

And the girl was always pretty. She was instructed to flirt with them and make them nice coffee. So I started to make a lot of money. And for about six months, I was on top of the world, and I ordered a Bugatti Chiron for 4 million dollars.

AND THEN CORONA CAME.

.   .   .

So, I mean, I'm okay for money, of course. But then Corona came and shut me down because they've closed everything.

Romania is, and I probably shouldn't say it, completely corrupt from head to toe.

Now I have a very, very extensive network in Romania. I like to make this very clear.

One of the reasons I love living there so much is because I'm at the very top echelon of society.

If I need to speak to the Prime Minister, I can make that happen. I can't do that in West.

So we went and met with some members of Parliament, and they're like, well, it's not us it's The European Union directing all this Covid lockdown garbage. They knew Covid was a scam. They knew it. Everyone knew it.

The European Union gave them billions in relief funds, or in reality, bribes to do it. So we can't really open the casinos.

Then I did a deal with them to open them on the sly and pay bribes. I was open for the first month with bribes, but the bribe kept going up because this is Romania, right?

THE POLICE CHIEF WOULD COME. He wants some. And the police chief would call his mate.

His mate is the fucking, I don't know, fire Inspector. Some Jackass. He'd come.

Then the alcohol licensing man would come. It was just like everyone was on the phone to each other, "Hey, this casino is still open. They'll pay you to go away". So before you know it, every five minutes, someone's at the door for money, and we weren't making money. So we had to close down.

And nobody feels sorry for the casino owner. It's kind of hard to play the pity card. My business has gone under, like, who gives a shit? Fuck you! You've got a Chiron. So I'm just stuck here right now. But I'm still living my life, traveling the world, driving my cars.

And if you took it all away from me now, I would start to make progress again. If I lost everything today back to flat zero? By tomorrow, I'd be making some progress. Even if I had £1 as opposed to zero.

As long as I feel like I'm doing something, I'm happy. This is how life works, right?

Let's take cars. You're driving at 200 miles an hour. You don't feel it. It's the accelerating part to 200 miles an hour that you feel. You don't feel it once you're doing the speed. You feel the acceleration. It's the acceleration that's exciting. You need to feel the change in your life to benefit from it.

I think the most miserable people on Earth are those people who are born filthy rich.

Imagine being born as an oil sheik. Money has no value. A Ferrari is not going to make you happy? It has no value. Nothing has value. Everything is just, whatever.

Girls have no value. You can buy unlimited hookers. You can buy unlimited Bugattis, whatever you want. Diamonds. It doesn't mean anything.

You have to be broke to appreciate being rich. You need that. So anyone who's sitting here thinking they want money. Good.

You need to feel how you feel now. Being poor is what's gonna make you happy once you have money.

This is a very key element to it, because I think it's the journey, not the destination. So there's still a whole bunch more for me to fucking waste money on.

∿

Star Wars

I really upset the Star Wars fans, because I made a point that I've never watched Star Wars. And every time I say I've never watched Star Wars, people are like, "Oh, you have to see it, you're missing out".

And I reply that I've lived a very good life, and I'm a multi-millionaire, retired world champion kickboxer. I feel like *they've* missed out.

That was the point I was trying to make. I don't need the movie. And I tweeted this statement out with a photo of me standing next to my Bentley

And everyone's commenting "That's not your car!" And it blew up in the geek world of Star Wars, right? All the geeks of the world hate me.

PERHAPS THERE'S JEALOUSY, but from a Karma perspective, I do believe that if you're good to people in general, in 99% of cases, if you show people respect, they show it back.

And a lot of people comment on this about me. I didn't even realise how overt I was until someone mentioned it, but i'm always super nice to wait staff. I tip massively.

I'm a very positive person. No one has a negative interaction with me unless it's genuinely a beef. I try my very, very best to come in and say hello to everybody.

If I'm at a hotel and I'm eating at a buffet, I'll finish the buffet and I'll go to the chef and say, that was amazing. Very good. Who's ever complimented a buffet chef? Nobody. They stand there all day cooking. Some fucking Egyptian dude. Making very average food.

And so I'll eat his average-ass food and then go tell him he's done a good job, and his face will light up like you would not believe.

I really believe in spreading positivity as a whole. I do believe in that. I don't see any reason to be negative. I mean, I'm sure the people who hate me think i'm full of shit. But I don't need to lie about anything I've ever done. I don't need to lie about the life I live.

I don't need to lie about my interactions with females, the money I make or anything. And what's really interesting to me is I now am getting more well known, I get recognised all the time.

When I was in America, I got recognised on the street. Usually from Instagram or from my YouTube channels, etc.

And there's two kinds of people. There's people who are jealous of me, and angry about what I say. And then there's the people who say, "Can you teach me something?"

Those are the smart ones, right? If there's someone who has something I want, even if I don't like him, I would think, "Well, he must know something that's useful to me. Is it better for me to make friends with this person and try and learn from him, or leave a hateful comment on his YouTube?

What's gonna benefit my life?" Do you understand what I mean? Because I'm not gonna read the hateful comment. What are you typing it for? I got shit to do. I'm too busy driving a Bugatti, bro!

It's very low IQ thing to sit there and think, "I'm jealous. I hate this guy". That's what a stupid person would do.

I could disagree with every single element of what some-body says, but if I believe that I can benefit from interaction with that person, then I'd make sure it's an amicable interaction.

People are just stupid. I mean, still to this day I get emails about the Star Wars thing, which is a year and a half ago. About three emails a day from some autistic crazy guy threatening to kill me over Star Wars.

The world is weird.

Social Media

I think it's simultaneously the biggest opportunity on the planet, and the ruination of the world.

I was watching American Pie the other Day. Remember that movie, American Pie?

Don't you think that was the happiest period in human history? Look at the party in that film. No one's on their phone. Everyone's at the party, involved in the party, they're talking to their friends. Maybe I'm an old man just thinking about the olden days. Back then you could text someone if you really had to, but no one's glued to their screen.

It was still the modern world, but without all this addiction.

I'm absolutely addicted to my phone. I'm not gonna lie. I'm a complete phone addict. I live on my phone. I'm always texting, all the time. There's always something going on. So I'm a phone addict. I know I've got a problem. But I was watching American Pie, and I was thinking, wasn't that a happy period of history?

You know, I think social media is the number one cause of depression.

If you're living a normal life and you scroll Instagram, you're gonna end up depressed. You're gonna see me with my Bugatti. You'll see some bitch on a boat, some other dude in the Maldives. You see all this fucking shit, and you're gonna look around your council flat in fucking County Durham and think "Fuck my life!"

You know, Instagram is depressing. Unless you're at the very, very top echelons of life, it's depressing.

Social media is a big reason that people are unhappy and depressed. It really does depress people.

But on top of that, it is the biggest opportunity in the world. Look at all the people you can reach and interact with via social media. So it can either ruin your life or it can make your life. So I think that if you're on social media, you need to be very, very careful about how you are using it.

And I always say to people who tell me social media depresses them, that they need to be producing for social media, not consuming. I really try very, very hard to put my Instagram picture up and then never read the comments. I never scroll the discovery feed. I don't look at anyone else's shit. I just try and post my own thing.

And I think if you do it that way, you can benefit from it. But if you sit there and you find yourself wasting an hour just consuming, I think it's an easy path to self destruction.

I have quite a big Instagram. 300,000 or so followers and a blue tick. I've got McLarens and Lambos, and all that shit in the photos.

Do I get girls hit me up on Instagram? Truthfully, not really. The odd one or two, but, I mean, it depends. There's certain places in the world that happens.

If I go to Dubai and I tag myself in Dubai, I start getting loads of DMs from girls who are not in Dubai, but who want to go, hoping I will fly them there and put them in a hotel.

I'll get a message saying "Oh, my God. I can't wait to go back to Dubai", and I'll ask "Well, when are you coming?" And they say, "Oh, I'm in Rio, I'm just trying to find a way there". Her and her two friends basically just saying, fly me, please.

But I'm not that guy, because there's something I want to make very, very clear: After you've lived my life... The Pimp, you can never go to being the customer. I can't be the customer. I can't pay for sex.

If a girl genuinely loves me, of course I'll take care of her flight. But I'm not gonna fly some random bitch over and put her up in a five star hotel just for a bit of sex.

I can't do that as a man because I don't want to ever feel pimped. I *was* the pimp. I won't enjoy that interaction. I can't do that. I can't be a customer. I'm a terrible sugar daddy target. But when I know you actually love me, then of course I'll take care of you.

But if you're like, "Oh, buy me this handbag", I'm gonna say "Fuck you!" It's not about the money to me. Of course I can afford it. It's just "Fuck you, you don't deserve it".

So a couple of times I get that kind of thing. But in general, not really.

In fact, I would actually say I'm too overt on social media. I think I put a lot of girls off. When I was less well known with about 40,000 followers it was a lot calmer.

Now they look at my page and think "No way on God's green Earth is this man gonna settle down and marry me. He's just gonna fucking run around and bang everything that moves". So I think I've gone too far with the socials.

You know, they talk about women's intuition. It's real. Women's intuition is a real thing.

They've evolved with it. They've evolved to sense danger. Women have evolved to tell if you're a creepy weirdo. It's a preservation strategy. Women can talk to you for a few seconds and think " Something's wrong with him. He's odd". They're good at detecting things. I know that's a bit cliche, but if you come across as genuinely confident, and they can genuinely feel a good vibe from you that's not creepy....

Then you can say anything.

I think you can go up to a go to girl say "Excuse me. Sorry to interrupt, I just want to say you are absolutely beautiful." And if you say it in a way that's calm, and nice and cool when you approach, they're gonna be okay with it.

I don't think you have to say anything fancy. But if you walk over and go "Ohhh, ummm", and you fuck it up; then you're a weirdo. So it's all about the delivery. I think that's how it kind of works.

~

Levels Of The Pimp Game

A pimp, is a Positively Inspirational and Motivating Person. Why would a woman work for a pimp? Why would a woman work for a pimp as opposed to just doing it by herself?

See, here's the thing. Everyone thinks it's fear, because they can't think of any other reason why a woman would give her money away. They must be scared of this man.

It's absolutely and utterly the complete opposite. This whole idea of pimping through fear is just movie bullshit. In the industry, they call it gorilla pimping. Gorilla pimping is when you scare a girl. How long can you scare a girl into giving you all her money. Years?

No, she's gonna leave. She's gonna run off. She's gonna call the police on you. You're gonna have trouble. You can't do that shit and stay out of jail. Maybe if you're a crack dealer and she is a crack head at the very, very bottom of the game. But you're not gonna be scaring a nice young 19 year old with a loving family at home to give you all her money. That's just not real. So it's never fear. It's the absolute complete opposite of fear. It's safety.

They feel safer working for you than they do by themselves.

So even with webcam, they feel safer working for me than they would by themselves. If a girl is doing it by herself and the computer fucks up, she can't fix it. If the taxman calls, she can't fix it. If she has a bad day online, maybe she starts feeling self conscious. She got her tits out and nobody paid attention to her.

Now. she doesn't want to do this anymore. If she works for me and says she had a bad day online, I'd say, "Oh, no, that's not your fault, there's a huge football game on. Yeah, it's massive. The whole website is dead. In fact, you did the best. All the other girls did really bad. You did the best".

Really? It's all a complete lie. There's no football game. She didn't do the best. She did shit. But it's fine now because she feels happy. I fixed the problem. You're a problem solver. It's better for her to give away a percentage to not have to worry about all this shit out there in the world.

Her job becomes very simple if she works for a man. She just performs X amount of hours. She does what she's supposed to do. And all the other stuff, the money into the bank, all the tax, all the problems, it's all fixed.

"Oh, this crazy customer found my real name!". "Don't worry, baby. I'll deal with them". "What are you going to do?", "Don't worry. I'll deal with him".

I'll just block him from the website. I won't even do anything. She'll think I went mafia on his ass.

It's a game, right? So it's never fear. It's safety. There was never a girl who worked for me who was afraid of me. They felt safe with me.

And what's really interesting, and it's gonna really piss the feminists off, but I'll tell you, it's the truth: It doesn't matter whether a woman wants to be a lawyer or a house maker or a webcam girl. Unless she has a man directing her, she's gonna fuck it up.

They're just not built to be completely independent creatures. The women who go, "I'm strong and independent." They're working for a man in a company and getting fucked by ten men a month. You're not independent. It is a lie. You're just undesirable. It's what you are.

There's no such thing as an independent female. They're all relying on a man to some degree. And if a woman wants to be very, very successful in her life, no matter what it is, whether she wants to be a gymnast or whatever she wants to be, at some point, there's a man in charge telling her what to do.

If you want to be the best webcam girl in the world, you want to make 50 grand a month, you need a man to make sure you do it right.

And another reason that they work for a man is because women are intrinsically lazy. If you show a woman how to make a $1,000 in an hour, she'll think "I can work 2 hours a week".

If you sure man how to make a $1,000 in an hour. He thinks "I can make $18,000 a day". We think about the world different.

So the girls that worked for me, I'd make their ass do their shifts, and they'd make a bunch of money. So this is just a dynamic. The dynamic is beneficial for everybody. A woman will never work for a pimp out of fear. Never. That whole view on it is wrong. It's completely wrong.

ALL RIGHT, so how many levels are there in the pimp game? That's a good question.

I would not consider myself at the top of the game. Because you know who's at the top of the pimp game? Every other job out here besides me.

If a girl worked for me, she got 20% of the money. Do you think the person working for McDonalds gets 20% of the money she rings up in the till? You think the person working for Starbucks is getting 20% of the money they ring up? They're getting less than 1%.

That's pimping. They'll make your stand your ass up

behind a fucking till all day in the heat, flipping burgers for minimum wage. They're taking in thousands and thousands of dollars in an hour, and then gonna pay you $7 an hour. That's real pimping.

Don't worry about what Tate's doing. He's buying the girl's Gucci handbags, and giving her 20% of his turnover. I'm a shit pimp. I'm terrible. All these businesses out here, they're the kings of pimping.

You know what real pimping is? A government locking you in your house, letting you go broke, lose your company, and your children are gonna starve. But it's for your safety because you might catch the common cold. That's pimping.

I'm very low down the scale, my friend. There are much higher levels than me. This whole world is a pimp game.

There's two kinds of people. There's pimps and tricks. That's all it is. You're either the pimp or you're being pimped.

I took women who were getting exploited in a normal job, and told them they can put a bra on and become rich, and get paid thousands.

I was nothing but a philanthropist. I'm nothing but a feminist. I promote women to be the best they can possibly be. I'm a terrible pimp. All these other jobs out here are pimping.

The BBC when it convinces women to not have children, and to dedicate their lives to some bullshit career in PR, that's pimping.

I never installed a frame in a woman's mind that was negative. I never taught her to do anything, or be anything, or think anything that was going to be detrimental to her life.

I made sure every single action she took benefited her, and benefited her bank account. I've never done anything bad to anybody.

A lot of people go, "Oh, yeah, but you exploited them". Listen, we can walk across there to that McDonald's and then you can talk about exploitation.

I'm a shit pimp.

~

Lessons And Material Things

I've lived a very, very eclectic life. And I really believe that the key to my experiences and the key to how I view the world is the fact that I've lived such an eclectic life.

I have had such different experiences. I've been broke, I've been a millionaire, I've been a pimp, I've been a fighter. I've done so many different things, and I really think that it's the contrast that makes life interesting. I'm happy with every single element of my life.

And even if I wasn't, I would refuse to admit that I'm not. This is the life I've lived. I accept all of it. If I've made a mistake in the past, it was the best thing I believed I should do at the time. This is another thing about people. It's kind of weird on my YouTube channel I talk a lot about, like, mental rigidity and these kind of things. And I get a lot of people messaging me saying they're very depressed.

Maybe they made this big mistake two years ago, and their wife left them. Whatever. And I try and explain to them that if you did what you believed was best at the time, then what are you mad for? Every mistake I made in my life at the time, I thought I was doing the right thing.

So I'm not going to be mad at past me. Every single bad thing that's happened to me, every single piece of trauma that's happened in my life has led me here. So if you're happy with where you are currently, then you have to be happy for every bad thing that's ever happened to you.

Genuinely. If you look at your life now and go, I'm quite happy with where I am. Then you have to be happy with every single shit day you've had because you wouldn't end up here any other way.

You know, I wouldn't have grown as a man if my father didn't die. You learn a lot about yourself as a man when your father dies. So of course, I wish my father was alive. But if I'm happy with my life now and where it is, you have to accept every shitty day and every single lesson.

So yeah, I'm happy for all of it. The good and the bad, my friend. I'm smiling, I'm breathing, I'm alive. And there's a whole bunch of people out here in the world today, who are not gonna be breathing by the end of it. There are a whole bunch of people in the world today who are gonna have a distraught day. Something shit is gonna happen. They're gonna be in a car crash. As long as that shit isn't happening to me, I am smiling. You cannot depress me. You can't piss on my Cheerios.

So all this material stuff like cars, the mansions, all the girls, it means nothing. I'd much rather see my father again. A thousand percent. Not even fucking close. It's not even close. I'd give up absolutely everything to be with him.

But you know, it's funny.... I'll tell you a story about his funeral. My Dad died when I was in Romania, and I had just moved my business there from London. And I was in this apartment with six girls, and we were supposed to be working. And I just bought all new equipment so we were all ready to get started. This is before I got big big. So I had only a little money. But I spent all of it setting up the business.

And then my Dad died, of course. So then I was supposed to go to his funeral. I was going to have to get up and leave Romania, fly all the way to Alabama, and stay in America for a few weeks. But then I knew by the time I came back, all the girls were going to quit or leave and all this kind of thing.

So I had to make a big decision. And I remember when I first started making my money, my Dad was still alive. The first thing I did with my money, the very first thing I did was retire my Mum. She told me how much she got paid at her job and I tripled it. She didn't have to work anymore.

Anyway, there I am having to make a choice whether I stay in Romania and focus on the business, or go to my Dad's funeral.

And I remember my Dad's lessons. My Dad would have been furious if I'd have fucked up the financial stability of the family, and of my mother and my brother just to go to his funeral.

My Dad knew I loved him. I spoke to him every single day. And from what he taught me, he's a chess player, he's a logical man, right?

Get your business running, then come to the grave, do it that way. So of course if I could give all this up now to get my dad back then of course I would. But I can't. So what's the best thing to do? Live without my father poor, or live without my father rich? I made the choice to miss his funeral, to take care of my mother, to build my empire. It's paid off fantastically.

To this day my mother is still retired. At the time she was cleaning dishes in the school kitchen in Luton, and now she gets to drive a nice car and live in Spain for most of the year. So I did the right thing. And I know my father if he's looking down on me, would be very, very proud of me because I made the logical decision.

So of course, there's things far more important than material things. I say this all the time because when you have money, people often think "Oh he has money, but he doesn't have anything else. All he has is money". Well for me there's not much above money. You have love of the people who you care about and who care about you. You have health, because nothing's worth anything if you're dying. There's no point being a billionaire if you're sick. So after love and health, what can't money buy? It's number three.

You know, money is extremely important. Trying to say money doesn't matter is a coping mechanism. It's a coping mechanism that poor people have so they don't shoot themselves in the head.

The smartest thing rich people ever did was come along and say to all the poor people, "Money doesn't make you happy. Don't worry. I'll keep all the money because it doesn't make you happy".

You never seen a rich man give his money away. No, they say money doesn't make you happy. "You keep slaving away for minimum wage. I'll stay over here a millionaire, but I'm not happy. So don't worry. Don't be jealous".

I know plenty of people out there who are millionaires who have a loving family, a loving wife and have perfect health. Their life is fantastic.

Just because you get money, it doesn't mean you lose the love of your family and shit. That's not true at all.

Feminists And Governments

The reason I upset feminists so much is because the typical feminist tactic is to cancel somebody.

To come at somebody and call them a misogynist, and those kind of things. And then that person loses their career or they get slandered. You can't slander me because I will state right now that I am absolutely sexist and I'm absolutely a misogynist. I have "fuck you" money and you can't take it away.

So I'll say what I want because I'm a realist. And when

you're a realist, you're sexist. There's no way you can be rooted in reality and not be sexist.

If you're about to get on a plane, and that plane's gonna fly through a hurricane, and there's 50/50 chance of crashing and dying. Do you want a male pilot or a female pilot?

To say a woman is such a politically correct answer. And it's a lie. We all know you'd want a man to fly that plane. You would not want some women to walk into the cockpit like "Hi, guys!".

Give me an old white haired man. Everyone knows it.

You're about to have brain surgery and there's a 3% chance of success. 97% chance you're gonna die. Are you more confident going to that operation seeing a man surgeon or a female surgeon?

We're all biased. We're all biased based on our experiences. I have seen so many women fail to park and crash cars, and do dumb shit.

I do not want a female pilot flying me through a hurricane. I've seen enough female driving of all vehicles to know that that shit is a bad idea. I want a male pilot.

AM I SEXIST? Yes.

Why? Because of my experiences of the world, I am a realist. I am absolutely and utterly a realist. And if you're a realist, you're sexist.

I believe women are better at some things, and men are better at other things. I do not believe we're equal and all the same and can be interchanged. I believe that certain roles suit females, and certain roles suit males.

Another scenario. Would you drop your child off in a day care where it was run only by men?

No. Women only. Of course

So there's a gender bias that exists.

And it's obviously a generalisation. But my point is, in

certain roles in society, we trust females, like working with our kids. And in other more dangerous roles, we trust men.

So I'm a "sexist". I'm a "misogynist". I'm misogynistic because I believe that females are weaker than men. That makes me a bad person in the feminists mind.

But if someone breaks in the house, I'm not sending her to fight.

It's my job, right? I have to risk my life to protect her.

So when someone isn't breaking in the house and I ask her for breakfast, I expect it to be made. These are the roles. These are the normal gender roles that got us here. People try and pretend that this is evil and bad.

The modern world was built on these traditional gender roles. The pyramids, going to the moon, the city of London, the fucking Suez Canal. Everything on the planet was built on the woman obeying the man in the family. That's how we got to this point.

This is the first time in history women have turned up and said, "We don't want to listen anymore", and everyone's pretending that that's a good thing. I'm not saying it's not. I'm saying we don't know. It's never been tested. We've never tested this new world where women don't want to listen to men at all.

They're all saying it's gonna lead to some Utopia. I personally don't believe that.

What's the statistical odds of every single society since the dawn of human time being led by men?

You have the Aztecs and the Mao Dynasty in Brazil and China. They never spoke. The idea couldn't spread, right. But just by coincidence, in every single society since the dawn of human time, the men were in charge.

What's the odds of that? So men are obviously designed to lead.

Now, I'm sure there was probably at some point in history, a female-led society that was tested. But the reason we don't discuss them is that they have no history, because they were annihilated and destroyed by the male-led societies. The male-lead societies are more efficient, and in the cold light of the world, and the brutal realities of life, efficiency wins.

So, the male-led societies are more efficient, they raise better armies, they build better cities. And when they find some fucking bunch of nancy boys run by women, they fuck them up and kill them so we never hear of them.

And we don't find any remains. There's no fucking cathedral to discover because they never built shit. Every single society that was successful since the dawn of human time was male-led, all of them. And then the last 30 years, we've come along and started saying, "Let's put women in charge. It's going to be good for us".

Well, I don't think it will be. And the problem is that this whole "women in charge" crap is Western.

The Chinese aren't putting women in charge. The Russians aren't putting women in charge. Do you think we're gonna stand around here letting women rule us, being a bunch of fucking cowards? The Chinese and Russians are gonna conquer the world. Let's talk in 100 years and I guarantee there'll be a history class. There'll be a history class where the Chinese say, "Do you remember when America just completely handed itself over to feminism and all this other crap and we just destroyed them in 20 short years?" That's what's gonna happen.

AND THEN THERE'S the whole LGBTQ crap.

Especially in schools. Leave the kids alone.

If you want to chop your dick off, I have nothing against that. I'm not anti gay. I'm not anti transgender. I'm not anti any of these things. What I am anti, is propagating your worldview on other people's children.

If you're gay and you can't have kids, why do you now believe it's your right to go to other people's kids and tell them how to think? If you've decided that the type of sex you want to have will prevent you from procreating, that's your decision, right?

You've decided that having sex with women isn't worth it for you. You don't want to have children. You want to have sex with other men. Fine. It's your decision and you're entitled to it.

That does not give you the right to go to other people's families; people who did decide to have children and raise them properly, and try and program their children.

Leave the kids alone. You can be as transgender as you like. But don't come talk to my kid about it. That's my child. I will program my child with my world views. I raise them. I pay for them. They're my kid. They're not your kid. And they're not the government's kid.

And this is what I was saying earlier about women being a blank slate. It's the same with children. You either program your woman and program your children, or society will do it.

Do you believe the lessons that society are teaching people today are good lessons? I don't. I will not send my kids to school. I don't think they're gonna learn anything.

I can teach them to fucking do maths at home. We have the Internet. We have unlimited information. I can tell them to Google World War Two and get them to write a report on it.

And with discipline, my kids will know more than any kid in any public school. Without the indoctrination, without all the fucking propaganda.

All this shit is very deliberate. Governments know what they're doing when they're trying to spread this propaganda.

And I think a lot of people do not understand yet. Because most people still live inside of the Matrix.

You are conditioned to go to school from 4 until 16, get a job, retire at 65. Shut up, do not question it.

. . .

WE'RE all scared to be different now. And as soon as you are different, people fucking point their fingers and want you back in your box. Then you have people identifying as pandas and shit.

It is insanity. And everyone knows it's insanity. But we're not supposed to say it's insanity.

A lot of people out here still amaze me. They believe the government cares about them. But the government doesn't give a fuck. Look at this Corona bullshit.

"Oh the government locked us in our house, but they want us safe". More people have died from missed doctor's appointments for cancer diagnosis than they did from Corona.

They don't want you safe. They never will care about you being safe. If you believe the government wants you safe, you are too far gone to save. What the government wants is slaves. Slavery has not gone anywhere.

Let's talk about slavery.

Governments in years past would get slaves, make them work for free, and build things. That's slavery. But they had to stop doing that.

So what do they do now? They get people, make them work and build things for money. But the government prints all the money.

So if a government can create as much as they want of something from thin air, and you'll give up your time and life for this thing, then you are still their slave. That's it.

Slaves before would work all day, and at the end, they got food and a house. Now you work all day, you get money, and you spend all your money on food and a house. Slavery is still here. They just put money in the middle.

Nothing's changed. And what they want are slaves who are gonna comply and pay their taxes. Plus whatever kind of indoctrination or societal programming they can instil inside of people to keep them doing that they're doing. Anything it takes to stop people waking up and realising, "Whoa, the government's fucking me here. I'm locked in my house. They've taken my business away. I'm paying how much tax?! What? They're helping me how much?"

If you actually wake up and look around you, you realise you're being destroyed in real time.

WE CAN TALK about this a lot because I understand money very well. This is what I do now. I gave up professional fighting to understand money.

I was having a conversation with someone the other day. They were talking about Joe Biden and his relief cheques. He gave out $1400 to all the people in America because of Corona. And they said, "Don't you think he's good, that he's helping the poor?" What!? Do you think that helps the poor?

Let's talk about this. You give 100 people a $1400 cheque. Everyone understands you can't just leave it in the bank forever because of inflation. The value goes down. Because that's what happens when they print trillions of dollars from the sky. The dollar becomes less valuable. And we're living in a world right now where inflation is getting out of control, especially in America in the last year, inflation's up like 6 or 7%.

So no poor person is gonna take that money and just leave it in the bank. They're gonna either spend it, or invest it.

Let's say there's 100 poor people, and these 100 poor people decide to spend their money.

Where do they spend it? In stores buying trainers and TVs and shit.

Who owns these businesses? Rich people. So now the rich people who own the businesses get the poor people's money.

Amazon, their stock price went up 30%. Why? Because

people were getting stimulus cheques and spending it on Amazon. It all went to the rich guy.

And then they go, "Oh yeah, but what about if they invest it?"

Invest it where? Invest it in the stock market? That increases the stock price. Who owns the company? Rich people. You've made them richer. It always ends up back with the rich people. You can't stop making the rich richer. You cannot stop it. People inside the Matrix don't understand what's happening. And they're gonna sit here and think that the government cares about them.

"Oh Biden gave me $1400". Listen, the government doesn't give a shit. The government is looking after it's friends. The government gave all the slaves a little bit of pocket money, so they can send it all to the rich guys. It's all a scam. And people inside of the Matrix do not understand.

It's all a scam. It's all a lie. The idea that the government cares about them is a lie. The government is never going to tell you anything that's going to wake you up. The government's gonna teach you things that are gonna make you subservient and compliant.

They're gonna allow all this crap about identifying as a panda, and all this other shit.

It is not an accident. When they can convince the average person on the street that some other person is a panda because they said so, then you are fully in the slave mindset. When it comes on the news that someone identifies as a panda, you have to agree they're a panda.

Otherwise you are a racist and a bigot and you get cancelled. You are done. You are now in full slave mode and that's what they want.

So you will continue to work your shit job, for shit money, while they continue to do whatever the fuck they like. It's all a scam.

. . .

LET ME TELL YOU SOMETHING... When this Corona thing was going on, I tried to fly to London from Romania. I had to fly on Wiz Air .

You can't get first class flights around Europe. It is all just low-cost carriers.

So I'm flying Wiz Air. I have a mask on. "Excuse me, Sir. Put the mask over your nose." It's this fucking air stewardess. Some minimum-wage bitch. So I put my mask over my nose. Everyone was freaking out about masks. I had to fill in all these home office papers when I landed. All this crap PCR tests, bla bla bla.

I decided that i'm not doing that again.

So about two months later, I flew on a private plane. There was no mask, no PCR tests, no home office paperwork. My pilots weren't wearing masks. And when I landed in the UK at Biggin Hill Airport, the people who met me in the BMW on the tarmac had no masks. Nobody had a mask on, and no one asked me to fill in shit.

You know why? Because I was rich.

Corona doesn't exist for the rich people. As soon as you pay 50 grand for a flight, they don't trouble you.

But they trouble the shit-muncher on the Wiz air flight. It's all a fucking scam.

All of it is a scam. And this is how the whole world has always worked and always will work. The people at the bottom just don't seem to get it. They don't seem to wake up. And they won't wake up because the people in charge try very hard to keep them asleep.

If you had a whole bunch of people who were your slaves, why would you tell them the truth about the world? Why would you do that? No.

When's the last time you went to school and learned how

money works, or banks work, or taxes, or any of the things that they use to control you? Never.

Instead they teach you about fucking photosynthesis. They don't want you to know anything. They just want you to sit and agree that 'Okay, he's a panda, and I stay in my house cause of Corona, and don't forget to clap for the NHS.

Like a performing seal. Like an idiot. People are idiots.

AND THEN THEY come to me and ask, "Tate, how did you make all this money"?

I opened my fucking eyes.

I looked around me. I started to think. Things that people never seem to do.

I don't know how they live in a dream for so fucking long. I woke up out of the dream, right? But this is the truth. Governments are absolutely the enemy of the people. They always have been. They always fucking will be. Fuck all of them.

Life And Depression

I think that every single person should be aiming to reproduce. And I think the most important thing anyone can do in their life is to have children. I'm super pro-children.

When I speak to some of these feminists, spouting "I don't want kids", I think you are the most miserable, stupid bitch in the world.

You're born with this gift to create life. And you think it's more important to eat microwave dinners, make 40 grand a year, and talk about your career. You're an idiot.

I think that truly you live forever through your genes, and through your blood.

And for me, how am I on the planet? It's because i've had a whole bunch of ancestors who worked very hard to stay alive for me to exist. They were dodging sabre-tooth tigers and shit. I think about my bloodline, all the crap they've been through just to get to this one point at the end.

So I can't have an attitude of, "I don't want kids, I wanna play video games. I want to be a feminist."

We're on the planet to reproduce. And I think we all have lessons to learn and teach our children. I think that's the most important thing we can do. I don't think there's anything more important than that. I know it's a bit boring but I think that's basically it. Stay alive and reproduce.

It's the first thing I think when I see someone committed suicide or something. I understand we all have trouble and bad things happen. I get it. I'm not saying I don't get it, but isn't that super disrespectful to your parents?

They went through all that shit to raise you, and now you're sad so you jump off a fucking bridge. If my kid did that, I'd be pissed. What a fucking moron! I wouldn't even give him a funeral.

I just think it's ultimately selfish. I think it's super, super selfish.

Like the guy from Linkin Park who killed himself. He has four kids.

I don't give a shit how bad your life is, bro with your millions. You idiot!

You have children. That should be reason enough to live, for anybody on the planet. I truly believe that.

I don't give a fuck what's going on in your life. If your kids are still breathing, you've got a fucking job to do. And you're not a man if you're going to say "fuck them kids, I'm sad".

Then you're a dick head as far as I'm concerned. So I believe we all have a duty to our bloodline and a duty to our ancestors.

And that duty is to reproduce the best we can, and to put a ripple in the pond of reality. To put a tear in the fabric of Earth.

This is why I try and live my life the way I do. I want to make an impact on people. I don't care if they read this and think "I fucking hate that guy". It doesn't matter because I've said things they'll at least remember, even for all the wrong reasons. I think the more of us that try and put a bend in space-time, I think the better the world will be as a whole.

AND OF COURSE SUICIDE, especially for men, is on the rise. I'll tell you why: Because life's depressing as a man.

We talk about depression all the time but we don't talk about things being depressing. They're different things. I don't believe in depression. I do believe in depressing. The idea of clinical depression as a disease I reject absolutely, and I do not believe it. I believe that certain things can happen that will make you feel depressed. And I believe that it's an evolutionary instinct humans have to warn them that there's something they're unhappy about in their life.

If I went to jail now for the rest of my life, I'd be depressed.

I've not caught a disease. I've not caught depression. I'm just in a shit situation that's depressing me.

A lot of people say to me, "I can't get a girlfriend because I'm depressed". I say, "No, you're depressed because you can't get a girlfriend". They're different things, right? A lot of people are pretending depression is why their life is shit, when in reality it's the opposite. Their life is shit, which is why they're depressed.

And this idea that we propagate, that it's a disease you catch, and there's nothing you can do about it.

It strikes out of nowhere, and it's just gonna ruin your life. I don't believe that. I completely don't believe that. I believe that the number one cure for depression for 99% of people on the Earth is $10 million.

You find me someone depressed in the fucking ghetto in Glasgow, and let's give them a ton of money and watch his fucking face light up. Bollocks if you got a disease, my friend. You haven't got a disease, you're unhappy with your surroundings.

AND THE REASON men kill themselves is because, for the majority of men, life is depressing.

Days go by. Day by day, you're getting older. Your woman won't fuck you. You're too old to get another one. There's no milk in the fridge.

Fuck it, this is shit. My life's shit. I'm depressed. Well, duh, I'd be depressed too. That's not a disease. That's a shitty life. If you were George Clooney, you'd be fine, right?

I say this and they go, "Oh, so why do the celebrities talk about depression then? Why do the people in charge talk about depression when they have good lives?"

I'll tell you why. Because it's a control mechanism. Everything I told you all about slavery, everything I told you all about the people in charge, is the elites trying to keep the slaves in line.

Depression is one of the tools they use. If they convince you that depression is real, you are too busy living inside of your own mind and being selfish, to look around you and understand the real world.

Do you understand what I'm saying to you? Do you think that the people in charge are going to let someone become a Hollywood celebrity and have massive influence, and then let them say whatever they want?

No. They're going to tell them they have to talk about depression, mental illness, and they're gonna do it convincingly, pretending they care about it. They're going to promote it. They convince every sad person out there, that they cannot fix it. And there's nothing they can do about it.

So people stay sad and stay depressed, because if they start to wake up and feel happy they'll look around and realise that they're getting shafted.

So let's keep them all sad enough to not do anything about it, but well enough to still work. It's a control mechanism. Depression is used by the elites to keep the poor people oppressed. It's another mind trick. "You're all sad, it's okay. You can't help it."

It's bullshit. You can't tell me I'm fucking sad and you can't tell me I can't help it.

I don't care if you're Angelina Jolie or a doctor, whoever the fuck you are. You cannot tell me I can't control my mind. That I wouldn't be able to do anything about it. I reject that. I reject that absolutely. If I got depressed, I would fix it because I'm Andrew Tate.

It's all a control mechanism. And men are killing themselves because life for a man is harder than life for a woman. Most men live depressing lives.

Women have an innate value that prevents them from ever being truly depressed.

You can be the ugliest bitch in the world. But you can still go to a club tonight and get some dick. At least you can feel wanted for ten minutes by that fucking crazy Congolese dude who will bang anything.

For most men out here, they can't even feel wanted. Their wife left them, they're invisible to women. Their kids don't talk to them. They're just not wanted.

So of course, they're depressed. This is a unique situation that happens to men. This does not happen to women.

So of course, more men kill themselves. On top of that, society has huge burdens on men. You can be a woman in her forties and be broke. No one gives a shit. But if you're a man in his forties and you're broke, and you haven't got a fucking car... people would be like, "How the fuck did you fuck your life up, bro?"

Men are supposed to be smart. We're supposed to be rich. Supposed to be interesting. Got to have jokes. Got to have chat up lines, right? Gotta be charming. Gotta be cool. Experiences. Stories. We need to have a lot of shit to be an important man.

To be a woman, you need makeup.

If you're a hot woman, if you're truly beautiful, you don't need anything else. I've been on boats in Dubai with 19 year old Moldovan girls. The guy who owns that boat needed $100 million. That bitch just needed makeup. Same boat.

THAT'S how hard it is. Look at a game of chess. The King moves one square at a time. He has to really work his way across the board.

What does the Queen do? Zips here, zips there. Easy for a chick right?

If you're an ugly bitch, you might say "Oh, yeah, it's fine for the hot ones, but I'm an ugly one". Well, if you're an ugly bitch, fine. But to a lesser extent, you can still do the same thing. You can still go out down the high street, get a kebab and a shag and a pint. Done.

Women don't ever find themselves in a situation where they look around and think "I am actually completely alone".

AND THAT'S the worst thing that will happen to a person, True loneliness.

And that's why men kill themselves. And that's why it's super important that we stop teaching people that depression is something that can't be fixed. I say this all the time. Every single mental health month they're claiming that depression's the worst thing in the world.

It's not helping. It's doing the opposite. Stop telling people that they can't fix it. Stop telling them it's a disease that's not their fault. And start telling people, "Look, if you work hard, you can feel better. You're depressed now. But if you go to the gym and you work out and you train, you get a good body, you start getting social, you get some friends, go to some social clubs, start to meet people, start to do things, you will feel better".

That is far more healthy than talking about a disease we can't fix. Don't give them pills. The gym has been proven to fix more depression than antidepressants.

This is statistical. So when I claim depression isn't real, people say what you're saying is dangerous and you're gonna hurt people.

I'm trying to help people. I'm trying to wake people the fuck up. If you're reading this and you're depressed, go to the gym tomorrow morning, and I guarantee you no matter how depressed you are you will feel better.

If you're considering suicide, promise me this: Get six pack abs first. And by the time you get the six pack, you won't want to do it anymore. That's how it works. This is why not enough men are motivated enough.

And this is why I have to keep moving. This is why my achievements are never enough. I can never be depressed if I never slow down.

Speed is extremely important. Speed defies gravity. How does a plane fly through the air? Speed.

You're moving too fast to fall if you're always attacking life. If you're always doing things, if you're always making more money, if you're always traveling the world doing this, doing that.

Unhappiness can't catch you.

. . .

I'M ALWAYS LOOKING FORWARD to something. I wake up every day excited. I'll go do this today. I'll go do that today. And I very much live my life in a frame of not thinking "I have to do this", but instead "I get to do this". There's another thing that a lot of people make a mistake with.

It's a better way to look at life. "Oh, I have to go to work today".

Change your language. "I get to go to work today". Imagine you had no job. It'd be worse, right? Because otherwise you wouldn't be working. So you get to go to work. "Oh, I have to fix the car." At least you have a car. You get to fix your car. Lots of people don't have one. "Oh, I have to go get the kids". No, you get to go get the kids, because you have these beautiful children who love you.

You understand? The way people even use their own language is wrong.

The world can be framed. Maybe I'm completely crazy. Maybe I am full of shit . But the frames I've installed in my mind are all beneficial to me. So if that makes me crazy and full of shit, good, because I can't become depressed.

So you can sit there and tell me I'm full of shit while you're depressed and I'm happy. I would never want to adopt the thinking of a depressed person. If you're depressed and tell me I'm full of shit, I don't want to think like you anyway.

I take it a day at a time, and I'm looking forward to all the stages of life.

When you're younger, you want to be crazy. When you're older, you want to be calm. I'm looking forward to being a granddad and all this other old stuff. I'm looking forward to all of it. I'm looking forward to telling my stories with a pipe and enjoying it.

Life changes as time goes on, and I think you need to

embrace it day by day. And I don't really have too much of a grand plan at this point.

A LOT of men take all the frames I used in my webcam business and apply it to their marriage. And they say their marriage has never been better. It's amazing, but unsurprising, because women are women and men are men.

But all in all, I genuinely want the best for everybody. And I look forward to speaking to a feminist.

I hope I can deprogram her and she can get her ass married, have some kids, make her man a dinner, and finally become a good woman and stop talking shit.

So I look forward to talking with a feminist. And I'll fix her brain. No problem.

∾

CORONA

I'm too fly for Corona,
I called a girl on the phona,
I tell her I'm a home owna,
No need for a loana.

Andrew Tate

~

Made in the USA
Coppell, TX
17 September 2022

83265610R00164